Westmoreland County, Virginia

Deeds and Wills

1768–1773

Deed Book 15

Abstracted by
Michael R. Marshall

Heritage Books
2023

HERITAGE BOOKS
AN IMPRINT OF HERITAGE BOOKS, INC.

Books, CDs, and more—Worldwide

For our listing of thousands of titles see our website
at
www.HeritageBooks.com

Published 2023 by
HERITAGE BOOKS, INC.
Publishing Division
5810 Ruatan Street
Berwyn Heights, MD 20740

Heritage Books by the author:

Westmoreland County, Virginia Deeds and Wills: Deed Book 12 [Part 3], 1754–1756 and Deed Book 13, 1756–1761

Westmoreland County, Virginia Deeds and Wills: Deed Book 14, 1761–1768

Westmoreland County, Virginia Deeds and Wills: Deed Book 15, 1768–1773

International Standard Book Number
Paperbound: 978-0-7884-2233-1

INTRODUCTION

Deed and will books can contain land transactions, mortgages, leases, bills of sale, power of attorney, marriage contracts, estate settlements, and much more information of genealogical interest. They are a must for researching your family history.

The volume contains entries from Westmoreland County Deed and Will Book No.15, 1768-1773 beginning on page 1 and ending on page 298 for Courts held November 29, 1768 through September 28, 1773.

An every-name index adds to the value of this work.

Notes with parenthesis "[ ]" contain additional information or clarification.

Spelling of names and places were cross-checked against the following publications for accuracy.

- Colonial Lands and Roads of Westmoreland County, Virginia; [Edward J. White] 2020
- Lands and Lesser Gentry of Eastern Westmoreland County, Virginia 1650-1840s, [Edward J. White] 2014),
- Historical Atlas of Westmoreland County, Virginia; [David Wolfe Eaton] 1942

Page 1.

Ann Butler's Will

In the name of God, Amen, I Ann Butler of Westmoreland County and Parish of Washington being sick and weak but of perfect mind, sense and memory do make and ordain this my last will and testament.

Item I leave the use of Negro girl Betty to my daughter Elizabeth Sanford during her natural life and after her decease to her son William Sanford provided that the said William Sanford shall give his sister Frances Sanford the first child the said Negro brings that shall live to be three years old; or on his refusal to let his sister have the child or to pay her 25 pounds cash in lieu thereof that the said Negro girl so given shall go to the heir at law.

Item I give to my granddaughter Sarah Stewart, Negro girl Lucy provided that she gives Lucy's first child that lives to three years old to her sister Isabel Butler, or on their refusal, 25 pounds cash.

Item I leave to my daughter Mary Sanford the use of two Negroes; David and Milly during her natural life and after her decease to be equally divided amongst her children.

Item I give to my granddaughter Ann Sanford, Negro girl Winney to receive her at 16 years or day of marriage, then to be equally divided between her children.

Item I give to my grandson John Butler, Negro girl Patt to receive her at the age of 20 years, the said Patt to be in the possession of my daughter Mary Sanford till he comes to that age and the first child. That the said Patt shall have that [child that] lives to be 3 years old to go to his brother William Butler, or on his refusal to pay him 25 pounds.

Item I lend to my granddaughter Ann Sanford the use of our Negro woman Bess for and during her natural life and after her decease the said wench I give to be divided amongst her children, only the first child the said Bess has, to go to my grandson William Butler, son of James Butler and if she refuses to let him have it that then to pay him 25 pounds cash.

Item I give to my loving friend Hannah Harrison 50 shillings to assist her in buying a saddle

Item I give to my friend Ann Harrison daughter of Lovell Harrison my saddle and bridle.

Item I give my wearing apparel both made and unmade to be equally divided between my daughters Mary Sanford and Elizabeth Sanford.

Item I give and bequeath to my daughter Mary Sanford one choice bed and furniture, one yoke of oxen, and my cart.

Item it is my will that all the rest of my estate not before given and after my debts and legacy's paid shall be equally divided between my son-in-law Willoughby Sanford and my grandson James Butler and my grandson William Butler son of James Butler.

Item it is my will and I do confirm it that if any of my grandchildren to whom I have left a Negro girl should refuse to give their first child as devised at three years old or the money that then any so refusing shall have no right, but it shall descend to the heirs at law.

Item and lastly, I do constitute and appoint my son-in-law Willoughby Sanford and my grandson James Butler my whole and sole executors of this my last will and testament. In witness whereof I have hereunto set my hand and seal this 13th day of September 1763.

Signed sealed and delivered in the presence of us Ann Butler (her mark)

Lovell Massey

Rachel Williams

Daniel Moxley

At a court held for Westmoreland County the 29th day of November 1768, this will was proved according to law by the oaths of Lovell Massey and Daniel Moxley witnesses thereto and ordered to be recorded and on the motion of Willoughby Sanford one of the executors therein named who made oath thereto according to law and together with Daniel Moxley his security entered into and acknowledged bond with condition as the law directs, certificate is granted him for obtaining a probate thereof in due form; liberty being reserved to James Butler the other executor to join in the probate when he shall think fit. Teste

Page 3.

Kirk to Berryman Indenture

This indenture made the 20th day of September 1768 between William Berryman of the County of Westmoreland and Parish of Washington of the one part and Jeremiah Kirk of the said parish and county of the other part. Witnesseth that Jeremiah Kirk in consideration of the 68 pounds 10 shillings current money of Virginia has sold unto William Berryman all that tract lying in the said parish and county aforesaid containing by estimation 100 acres being a tract of land formerly belonging to Mr. Robert Washington, Gent., and by the said Washington sold to William Hutcheson of the said county and parish and whereas the said Hutcheson hath by his last will and testament left the above said land to be sold and hath directed and empowered his executors to sell the said land at 18 months credit the said Jeremiah Kirk being grandfather to the said Hutcheson's daughter took upon him the executorship and in order to fulfill the desire and intent of the testator advertised the said land to be sold to the highest bidder was the said William Berryman, which said land lies in the Irish Neck adjoining the lands of the said Berryman, McCarty and Lovell Massey butting up to the pond which falls into Rozier's Creek and along Major Thomas Vivion's land which he bought of James Lovell and so along the said Vivion's line to the Irish Neck Road to the said Berryman's land which he bought of Robert Lovell and John Lovell. In witness whereof [xxxxxxxxx] hath hereunto set their hand and seal the day and year above written.
Signed sealed and delivered in presence of Jeremiah Kirk
Lovell Massey, Benjamin Stuart
George Monroe, James Degges
Edward Promfrett, Reuben Grigsby
At a court held for Westmoreland County the 29th day of November 1768 this indenture together with the memorandum of livery of seizen thereunder written and the receipt endorsed were proved by the oath of Lovell Massey, Benjamin Stuart and Edward Promfrett witnesses thereto and ordered to be recorded. Teste

Page 5.

Ruth Read's Will

In the name of God, Amen, Ruth Read of Westmoreland County and Cople Parish, planter being weak of body of perfect sense and memory do make this my last will and testament in manner and form following.
It is my will and desire that my husband's estate shall be fully made up which is 60 pounds and the remaining part of my estate which is not disposed of I give to my daughter Mary Read and my grandson Andrew Read.
I give two parts of my estate which is not disposed of and the remainder to my grandson Andrew Read to them and their heirs forever.
Given under my hand this 4th day of October 1768
Signed and sealed in presence of us Ruth Read
John Hutt, Spencer Gill
At a court held for Westmoreland County the 29th day of November 1768 this will was proved according to law by the oath of John Hutt and Spencer Gill witnesses thereto and ordered to be recorded and no executors being named in the said will, on the motion of Andrew Read who made oath to the said will according to law and together with John Hutt and Richard Parker their securities entered into and acknowledged bond with condition as the law directs, certificate is granted them for obtaining letters of administration of the estate of the said Testatrix with the said will annexed in due form. Teste

Page 6.

John Naughty's Will

In the name of God, Amen, this 24th day of November 1768 I John Naughty of the County of Westmoreland though weak in body yet of sound and perfect mind and memory do constitute, make, and ordain this my last will and testament in manner and form following.

Imprimis, I leave to Martha Brown the use of my Negro wench Tamor and her son Clark, and my Negro wench Pegg during her natural life after her decease to be disposed of in the following manner;
Item I give and bequeath unto Mary Brown the above-mentioned Negro wench name Pegg to be possessed and enjoyed by her after her mother's decease.
Item I give and bequeath unto John Bridges, the son of the above-mentioned Martha Brown the other Negro wench named Tamor, and I give and bequeath likewise to his daughter Patty Bridges the above-mentioned Negro boy Clark to be possessed and enjoyed by them immediately after the decease of Martha Brown.
Item I give and bequeath unto Martha Brown, two of my best feather beds and the furniture belonging thereto, and likewise, the third part of my cattle, hogs and sheep, pot iron and pewter forever.
Item I give and bequeath unto James Thomas, Negro man Glasgow and a sorrel horse name Snip, and likewise a feather bed and furniture forever.
Item I give and bequeath unto Anne Garrard the daughter of William Garrard Negro boy Charles.
Item I give and bequeath unto my godson Yelverton Quisenberry, Negro boy Billy.
Item I give and bequeath unto John Berkley the son of William Berkley, my Negro girl Silvia.
Item I give and bequeath unto John Bridges my still and my desk, and all the wooden ware belonging to my estate.
Item I give and bequeath unto Mary Brown, Negro boy Ellick and one third part my pot iron and pewter; and likewise, a mare colt about two years old.
Item I give and bequeath unto my godson William Payne, 10 pounds currency.
Item I give and bequeath unto my godson John Bridges the son of William Bridges 10 pounds currency.
Item I give and bequeath unto my godson Richard Garrard the son of Nathaniel Garrard, 10 pounds currency.
Item I appoint, ordain, and constitute my friend George Payne and John Bridges to be my executors of this my last will and testament. In witness whereof I have hereunto set my hand and affixed my seal the day, month, and year first above written.
Signed sealed pushed and declared in presence of John Naughty
William Berkley
Edward Granger (his mark)
Elizabeth Granger (her mark)
At a court held for Westmoreland County the 29th day of November 1768 this will was proved according to law by the oath of William Berkley, Edward Granger, and Elizabeth Granger the witnesses thereto and ordered to be recorded; and on the motion of George Payne and John Bridges the executors in the said will named who made oath thereto according to law and together with John Bulger and Richard Muse their securities entered into and acknowledged bond with condition as the law directs, certificate is granted them for obtaining a probate thereof in due form. Teste

Page 8.
Dozier & Wife to Lawson Indenture
This indenture made the fourth day of October 1768 between Thomas Dozier and Sarah Dozier his wife of the Parish of Cople and County of Westmoreland of the one part and John Lawson of the Parish of Lunenburg and County of Richmond of the other part. Witnesseth that Thomas Dozier and Sarah Dozier his wife in consideration of 20 pounds lawful money of Virginia has sold unto John Lawson all that tract of land lying in the Parish of Cople and County of Westmoreland containing according to a survey made by Thomas Chilton, Gent., 25 acres, one rod and 30 poles, being part of a tract of land purchased by the said Thomas Dozier and his brother Richard Dozier of Sampson Damourvell and adjoining the land of the said John Lawson; beginning at a marked red oak standing in the line of the said John

Lawson and running along the same North 34° East 162 poles to a small marked white oak corner tree to the said Thomas Dozier and his brother Richard Dozier, thence North 75° West 17 ½ poles along the dividing line of the said Thomas Dozier and Richard Dozier to a small run, thence southwesterly along the meanders of the said run to where it forks, another small run falling into it, by or near a sweet gum, corner tree to this land and the land of William Thomas, thence, of the last mentioned run South 44 ½° West 12 poles to the foot of the hill near the said run, thence up the hill South 37 ½° East 18 ½ poles to a marked white oak corner tree to this said William Thomas, thence southwesterly to the beginning. In witness whereof we the said Thomas Dozier and Sarah Dozier his wife have hereunto set our hands and seals.
Signed sealed and delivered in presence of us Thomas Dozier
Alexander Spark, John Lyell
Samuel Eskridge
At a court held for Westmoreland County the 28th day of February 1769 this indenture was acknowledged by Thomas Dozier and Sarah Dozier his wife parties thereto (she being first privy examined as the law directs in order to be recorded. Teste

Page 10.
Tyler & Wife to Jones Indenture
This indenture made the ninth day of March 1769 between William Tyler of the County of Westmoreland and Esther Tyler his wife of the one part and Joseph Jones of the County of King George of the other part. Whereas William Tyler being largely indebted to James Miller of the town of Port Royal, the said James Miller commenced a suit at law for the recovery thereof and obtained a judgment an issued execution thereon by virtue of which said execution sundries slaves (to wit); Bob, Sue, Scipio, Harry, Mott, Taff, Joan, Nell, Ned, Sampson and Charles Nelson; 21 head of cattle, 20 head of hogs, one horse and one ferryboat were taken and exposed to sale and were purchased by the said Joseph Jones and whereas the said Joseph Jones hath agreed to continue the said slaves, stocks and other things upon the plantation of the said William Tyler towards the support of the family and the reimbursing the said Joseph Jones what the said William Tyler was indebted to the said James Miller in which by virtue of the purchase aforesaid the said Joseph Jones hath advanced unto the said James Miller and whereas the said William Tyler and Esther Tyler his wife have agreed to make over the said plantation unto the said Joseph Jones for the consideration thereon before mentioned. This indenture witnesseth that he the said William Tyler and Esther Tyler his wife for and in consideration of the sum of 1000 pounds of tobacco, 20 barrels of Indian corn, 20 bushels of wheat, 1000 pounds of pork to be paid and allowed the said William Tyler and Esther Tyler his wife annually during the life of the said William Tyler or until the said Joseph Jones shall be fully reimbursed what the said William Tyler doth now or shall during the said term owe and the indebted to the said Joseph Jones and granted, assigned, and set over, and by these presents do grant, assign and set over unto the said Joseph Jones and his heirs all that tract of land and premises whereon the said William Tyler now dwelleth, situate on the Potomac River containing by estimation 360 acres. To have and to hold the said tract of land and premises unto the said Joseph Jones for and during the term of the life of the said William Tyler or until the said Joseph Jones shall out of the profits to be made therefrom reimbursed himself what the said William Tyler now is or may hereafter be indebted to the said Joseph Jones. In witness whereof the said William Tyler and Esther Tyler his wife have hereunto set their hands and seals the day and year above written.
Sealed and delivered in presence of William Tyler
William Bernard
Spence Monroe
At a court continued and held for Westmoreland County the 30th day of March 1769 this indenture was proved by the oath of William Bernard, Gent., And Spence Monroe the witnesses thereto and ordered to be recorded. Teste

Page 11.
Pierce & Wife to Redman Indenture
This indenture made the 19th day of May 1769 between William Pierce of the Parish of Cople and County of Westmoreland and Sarah Pierce his wife of the one part and Solomon Redman of the same parish and county of the other part. Witnesseth that William Pierce and Sarah Pierce his wife in consideration of 97 pounds, 11 shillings and 3 pence current money have sold unto Solomon Redman all that tract of land lying in the parish and county aforesaid containing 111 ½ acres and bounded as followeth; beginning at a small gum corner tree to William Sturman's running thence South 27° West 15 poles to the mouth of a small branch, thence up the said branch North 56° West 13 4/10 poles, thence North 50° West 13 2/10 poles, thence North 31 ½° West 27 6/10 poles, to the head of a gully, thence North 51° West 50 poles, thence North 89° West 20 8/10 poles, to the head of a another branch, thence down the said branch to the main run of Rappahannock Creek, then up the said run it several meanders Vaulx's Mill Dam, and thence along a line of irregular marked trees dividing this land and that of William Sturman's, southeasterly to the gum at the first station, which said tract was sold and conveyed by the said William Pierce by William Black of the County of Prince George's [Maryland] as by indenture of sale bearing date the 24th day of June 1766. In witness whereof the said William Pierce and Sarah Pierce his wife have hereunto set their hands and seals the day and year above written.
Sealed and delivered in presence of — William Pierce
Hannah Washington — Sarah Pierce
Elizabeth Buckner
Richard Buckner
At a court held for Westmoreland County the 30th day of May 1769 this indenture was acknowledged by William Pierce and Sarah Pierce his wife parties thereto (she being first privy examined as the law directs) and the receipt endorsed was also acknowledged by the said William and together with the said indenture ordered to be recorded. Teste

Page 13.
Smith & Lee to Lee Indenture Tripartite
This indenture Tripartite made the 30th day of August 1768 between John Smith of the Parish of Wicomico and County of Northumberland, Gent., of the first part, Mary Lee of the Parish of Cople and County of Westmoreland, widow of the second part and John Lee of the Parish of St. Anne's and County of Essex, Gent., of the third part. Whereas a marriage by God's permission is intended shortly to be had and solemnized between the said John Smith and the said Mary Lee and whereas John Lee, late of the County of Essex, Gent., deceased did by his last will and testament in writing bearing date the 23rd day of September 1765, devised to his widow the said Mary Lee, party to these presents, the use of his lands in the said County of Westmoreland for and during her natural life and also sundry slaves and other personal estate and by the said will, appointed the said Mary Lee, the said John Lee and Richard Lee of the said County of Westmoreland, Gent., executors of the said will; and whereas the said Mary Lee only has taken upon herself the burthen of the execution of the said will, and whereas likewise the said Mary Lee since the death of her husband, the said John Lee hath acquired other estate consisting of slaves, stocks of cattle, horses, sheep and hogs, and other personal estate to a considerable amount, and whereas also the said John Lee, the late husband of the said Mary Lee, did very considerably indebted to sundry persons as well in Great Britain as in this colony and elsewhere, sundry of which debts are still due and unpaid. Now this indenture witnesseth that in consideration of the said intended marriage and likewise for the sum of five shillings to the said Mary Lee in hand paid by the said John Lee the receipt whereof is hereby acknowledged she the said Mary Lee hath given granted bargained and sold and by these presents doth give grant bargain and sell unto the said John Lee party to these presents, all the lands slaves stocks and other estate before

mentioned to be devised to her by her husband's will and also all other the estate of the said Mary Lee except her paraphernalia and wearing apparel. To have and to hold the premises aforesaid except as excepted unto the said John Lee his executors and administrators in trust to and for the several uses intents and purposes following; and first for the said John Lee to take all and every part of the said estate under his care and management and to apply the profits thereof towards the discharge of the debts the said John Lee, deceased and if the said John Lee party to these presents shall judge it necessary to sell and dispose of any part of the said estate then to sell and dispose of the same or such part thereof as he together with the said Mary Lee and John Smith shall judge most convenient in order to discharge fully the debts of the said John Lee, the testator agreeable to the intentions of his will. And also in trust to discharge such debts as the said Mary Lee has contracted since the death of her husband, and after the debts aforesaid are paid, then in trust to permit the same Mary Lee and John Smith, in case the marriage shall take effect, to receive the profits of the said estate during their joint lives and if the said Mary Lee shall survive the said John Smith then to the sole use of the said Mary in as full and ample manner as it is given her by the will of her late husband and as she enjoyed the same before this deed was executed. But if she should die under coverture in the lifetime of the said John Smith, then the whole of the estate herein before mentioned or intended to be bargained and sold for such part thereof as the said Mary Lee as an absolute property in, in trust to the use of such person or persons as the said Mary Lee shall by her last will and testament in writing or any deed in writing executed in the presence of two or more witnesses give or devise the same. And the said Mary Lee for herself her executors, administrators doth covenant promise and grant to and with the said John Lee his executors and administrators that the estate of the said John Smith shall not be liable for any part or parcel of the debts due from the said Mary Lee to any persons whatsoever. And the said John Smith for himself his heirs executors and administrators doth covenant promise and grant to and with the said John Lee his heirs executors and administrators that the estate of the said Mary Lee shall by no means be liable for any debts which the said John Smith owes at the time or may contract during his coverture with the said Mary Lee and he doth likewise covenant and grant to and with the said John Lee that it shall and may be lawful for the said Mary Lee to make such dispositions of her estate during coverture either by will or deeds in writing as aforesaid as she shall think proper without the molestation or hindrance of him the said John Smith. In witness whereof the parties to these presents have hereunto set their hands and seals the day and year first written.

Sealed and delivered in presence of us — John Smith
Thomas Smith — John Lee
Philip Smith
Solomon Robinson

At a court held for Westmoreland County the 30th day of May 1769 this indenture was proved by the oath of Thomas Smith, clerk a witness thereto and having been before proved by the oath of the other two witnesses thereto is ordered to be recorded. Teste.

Page 14.
<u>Balthrop to Kendall Indenture</u>
This indenture made the 21st day of January 1769 between William Balthrop of the County of Westmoreland of the one part and Woffendall Kendall of the same county of the other part. Witnesseth that William Balthrop in consideration of 80 pounds current money of Virginia has sold to Woffendall Kendall all that tract of land lying in the Parish of Washington and County of Westmoreland containing by estimation 270 acres; beginning at a corner tree adjoining to the lands of Thomas Pratt, thence down a branch to the Attopin Run, thence down the said run to the line of James White, from thence to the line of James Whitfield, and from thence to the line of John Wilkerson, thence along the said Wilkerson's line to the line of George Edwards, thence along Edwards line to the beginning. In testimony whereof the said William Balthrop as hereunto put his hand and seal the day and year above written.

Signed sealed and acknowledged in presence of William Balthrop
George White, John Wilkerson
Francis Lacey, Ben Wilkerson (his mark)
Robert Wilkerson (his mark)
At a court held for Westmoreland County that 30th day of May 1769 this indenture and the receipt underwritten were proved by the oaths of George White, John Wilkerson and Francis Lacey witnesses thereto and ordered to be recorded. Teste

Page 17.
Lee, Smith & Wife to Smith Indenture Tripartite
This indenture tripartite made the 13th day of January 1769 between John Lee of the County of Essex of the first part, Richard Lee of the County of Westmoreland, Esq. of the second part, and John Smith of the County of Northumberland, Esq. and Mary Smith his wife of the third part. Whereas John Lee, late of the County of Essex, Gent., deceased did by his last will and testament in writing bearing date the 23rd day of September 1765, devised to the said Mary his widow the use of all his lands in the County of Westmoreland for and during her natural life and after her decease a certain part thereof particular specified in the said will, to the said Richard Lee and his heirs forever; and whereas the said Mary has since intermarried with the said John Smith but before such intermarriage by indenture tripartite bearing date the 30th day of August 1768 made or mentioned to be made between John Smith aforesaid of the first part and the said Mary the second part and the said John Lee third part, conveyed the whole of the estate devised to her by the will of the said John Lee before mentioned on to the said John Lee, party to these presents and his heirs in trust among other things to take all and every part of the said estate under his care and management and to apply the profits thereof towards the discharge of the debts of the said John Lee, deceased, and if the said John Lee party hereto should judge it necessary to sell and dispose of any part of the said estate, then to sell and dispose of the same or such part thereof as he together with the said John Smith and Mary Smith his wife should judge most convenient in order to discharge fully debts of the said John Lee, the testator, agreeable to the intention of his will; and whereas it is found by the said John Lee party to these presents absolutely necessary for the purposes aforesaid to sell and dispose of the dividend of the tract of land devised as aforesaid to the said Richard Lee after the death of the said Mary and the said John Smith and Mary Smith his wife have given their assent thereto, which is testified by them becoming parties to these presents, now this indenture witnesseth that the said John Lee in consideration of the trust reposed in him and for the sum of 460 pounds to him in hand or secured to be paid by the said Richard Lee, the receipt whereof he doth hereby acknowledge, hath granted bargain sold and confirmed and by these presents doth grant bargain sell and confirm unto the said Richard Lee and his heirs and assigns all the said tract or parcel of land to him devised by the will aforesaid (after the death of the said Mary) to have and to hold the said tract or parcel of land with all the privileges and appurtenances thereunto belonging unto him the said Richard Lee his heirs and assigns forever against them the said John Smith and Mary Smith his wife, or either of them or the said John Lee, party hereto or his heirs. In witness whereof the said John Lee, John Smith and Mary Smith his wife have hereunto mutually set their hands and affixed their seals the day and year above written.
Sealed and delivered in presence of John Lee
Thomas Smith John Smith
G. L. Smith Mary Smith
Philip Smith
At a court held for Westmoreland County the 30th day of May 1769 this indenture and the receipt endorsed were proved by the oaths of Thomas Smith, clerk and John Augustine Washington witnesses thereto and having been before proved by the oath of Philip Smith another of the witnesses thereto are ordered to be recorded. Teste

Page 19.
Jeremiah Middleton's Will
In the name of God, Amen, I Jeremiah Middleton of Cople Parish and County of Westmoreland being sick and weak of body but of sound mind perfect sense and memory do make and ordain this my last will and testament as followeth.
Item I give and bequeath to my son John Middleton all the land I hold in the County of Westmoreland.
Item I give and bequeath to my son George Middleton of the land I hold in Richmond and Northumberland Counties.
Item I give to my son John Middleton, Negro girl Judea, and my gun.
Item I give to my son George Middleton, Negro girl Hannah.
I give all the rest of my estate to my beloved wife during her natural life, she not making willful waste thereof and after her decease to be equally divided between my four children and further my will and desire is that my loving wife be my whole and sole executrix of this my last will and testament. In witness whereof I have set my hand and seal this 26th day of December 1768.
Signed and sealed in presence of Jeremiah Middleton (his mark)
Robert Middleton, John Kesterson, Jr.
William Anderson, George Rust
At a court held for Westmoreland County the 30th day of May 1769 this will was proved according to law by the oath of John Kesterson, Jr. and William Anderson witnesses thereto and ordered to be recorded and on the motion of Sarah Ellen Middleton the executrix therein named who made oath thereto according to law together with Frances Wright and Daniel Bennett her securities entered into and acknowledged bond with condition as the law directs, certificate is granted for obtaining a probate thereof in due form. Teste.

Page 20.
Tyler to Tyler Lease
This indenture made the 9th day of October 1768 between Charles Tyler of Westmoreland County, planter of the one part and John Tyler of the said County of Westmoreland, planter of the other part. Witnesseth that Charles Tyler in consideration of five shillings sterling has assigned all that tract of land containing 226 acres lying in the County of Westmoreland, bounded south east land formerly belonging to Jarrett [Gerrard] Foard, Northeast with Potomack River, North Northwest with the land formerly belonging to Thomas Boyce, deceased, Southwest with the main woods. To have and to hold the said lands and all the appurtenances unto the said John Tyler from the day next before the day of the date thereof for and during the term of one whole year paying one pepper corn on the feast of Saint Michael the Archangel to the intent that by virtue of these presents and by force of the statute for transferring uses into possession the said John Tyler may be in actual possession of all and singular the said premises and hereby be enabled to accept take a grant and release of the reversion and inheritance is thereof. In witness whereof the said parties to these presents have hereunto interchangeably set their hands and seals the day and year above written.
Sealed and delivered in the presence of us Charles Tyler
Thomas Peach, Woffendall Kendall
George Kitchen, Stephen Bailey
John Atwood
At a court held for Westmoreland County the 30th day of May 1769 this indenture was proved by the oath of John Atwood a witness thereto and At a court held for the said county the 28th day of March last past the said indenture being proved by the oath of Woffendall Kendall and Stephen Bailey two other witnesses thereto is ordered to be recorded. Test

Page 22.
Tyler Release to Tyler
This indenture made the 10th day of October 1768 between Charles Tyler of the County of Westmoreland, Planter of the one part and John Tyler of the said County of Westmoreland of the other part. Whereas Charles Tyler in consideration of 271 pounds 4 shillings current money of Virginia has sold and released to Charles Tyler in his actual possession by virtue of a bargain and sale made for one year by indenture bearing date the day next before the date of this presence and force of the statute for transferring uses into possession, 226 acres lying in the County of Westmoreland, the said land being granted unto William Northall by patent dated 13th of March 1660 and was renewed 28 March 1662, bounded south east with the land formerly belonging to Gerrard Foard, Northeast with Potomack River, North Northwest with the land formerly belonging to Thomas Boyce, deceased, Southwest with the main woods, being the land whereon William Tyler now dwells.
In witness whereof the said parties to these presents have hereunto interchangeably set their hands and seals the day and year first before written.
Sealed and delivered in the presence of us Charles Tyler
Thomas Peach, Woffendall Kendall
George Kitchen, Stephen Bailey
John Atwood
At a court held for Westmoreland County the 30th day of May 1769 this indenture and the receipt endorsed was proved by the oath of John Atwood a witness thereto and At a court held for the said County the 28th day of March last past the said indenture and receipt being proved by the oath of Woffendall Kendall and Stephen Bailey two other witnesses thereto is ordered to be recorded. Test
Charles Tyler to John Tyler and John Tyler to Charles Tyler Performance Bonds follow on Page 25 and Page 26.

Page 27.
Rust & Wife to Rust Indenture
This indenture made the 30th day of May 1769 between Peter Rust and Rebecca Rust his wife of the Parish of Cople and County of Westmoreland of the one part and Samuel Rust of the same Parish and County of the other part. Witnesseth that Peter Rust and Rebecca Rust his wife in consideration of 104 pounds current money of Virginia has sold to Peter Rust all that land whereon Robert Newberry and Jeremiah Courtney now live and leased by James Courtney unto Ashton Hall and Jeremiah Courtney and containing by estimation 110 acres lying in Yeocomico Neck and the Parish of Cople and County of Westmoreland and bounded by the land of the said Samuel Rust that the said Samuel Rust purchased of Samuel Eskridge and by the creek known by the name of Earle's Creek and up a branch of the said creek that runs of between James Courtney and Jeremiah Courtney to the road that leads down into Yeocomico Neck and down the said road to the land of the said Samuel Rust that formerly was Eskridge's. In witness whereof the parties first mentioned to these presents have hereunto set their hands and seals the day and year first above written.
Signed sealed and delivered Peter Rust
John Pierce, Thomas Fisher Rebecca Rust
At a court held for Westmoreland County the 30th day of May 1769 this indenture and the receipt endorsed were acknowledged by Peter Rust already had thereto and ordered to be recorded. Teste

Page 27.
Rust to Rust Deed of Gift
I Samuel Rust of the Parish of Cople and County of Westmoreland in consideration of the natural love and affection which I have and bare unto my son Peter Rust and for the better maintenance and livelihood of him hath given unto him and his heirs forever the land I bought

of Presley Cox and Robert Jeffries situated in the aforesaid parish and containing by estimation 152 acres and bounded as followeth; beginning at a stone that formerly was Jeffries corner, from thence northeasterly to a large white oak standing by the road that goes to Yeocomico Warehouse, from thence along the line of Tebbs and Bailey down to Marsh Cove, and down the said called to the Back Creek, thence up the said creek and branch to the beginning stone. In witness whereof I have hereunto set my hand and seal this 30th day of May 1769.

Signed sealed and delivered in presence of us Samuel Rust
John Pierce
Thomas Fisher

At a court held for Westmoreland County the 30th day of May 1769 this indenture was acknowledged by Samuel Rust party thereto and ordered to be recorded. Test

Page 29.

Bernard to Pratt Indenture

This indenture made the 30th day of July 1768 between William Bernard of the County of Westmoreland of the one part and John Burkett Pratt of the County of Stafford of the other part. Witnesseth that William Bernard in consideration of 20 shillings has sold unto John Burkett Pratt one acre of land situate in Washington Parish and the County of Westmoreland on a run or stream of water called the South Branch of Machodoc Creek, beginning at a maple on the said run below the mill house, running thence South East 12 poles and six links of chain to a stake, thence South West 12 poles and six links of chain to another stake, thence North West 12 poles and six links of chain to another stake on the pond side, from thence to the beginning maple. In witness whereof the said William Bernard Hereunto set his hand and seal the year and day of the above written.

Signed sealed and delivered in presence of William Bernard

At a court held for Westmoreland County the 27th day of June 1769 this indenture and the receipt endorsed were acknowledged by William Bernard party thereto and ordered to be recorded. Teste

Page 31.

Jett & Bernard to Morris Indenture

This indenture made the 29th day of May 1769 between Thomas Jett of the County of King George and William Bernard of the County of Westmoreland, trustees of Francis Williams also of the County of Westmoreland of the one part and Charles Morris of the County of Westmoreland of the other part. Whereas Francis Williams by a certain indenture of bargain and sale did among other things sell unto Thomas Jett and William Bernard of parcel of land lying in the Parish of Washington and County of Westmoreland containing by estimation 400 acres in trust to be sold for the payment of his debts and whereas the said Thomas Jett and William Bernard in pursuance of the said trust did expose to sale the said tract of land and the said Charles Morris having offered 130 pounds which was the most that could be got. This indenture therefore witness that the said Thomas Jett and William Bernard in consequence thereof and in pursuance of the said trust in the said sum of money have sold by these presents unto Charles Morris the aforesaid tract of land and appurtenances thereunto belonging. In witness whereof the said Thomas Jett and William Bernard have hereunto set their hands and seals the day and year above mentioned.

Signed sealed and delivered in presence of Thomas Jett
William Bernard

At a court held for Westmoreland County the 29th day of August 1769 this indenture and the receipt annexed were acknowledged by Thomas Jett and William Bernard parties thereto and ordered to be recorded. Teste

Page 32.

Williams to Morris Indenture
This indenture made the 29th day of May 1769 between Francis Williamsof the County of Westmoreland of the one part and Charles Morris of the same county of the other part. Whereas Francis Williams heretofore by indenture of bargain and sale transferred unto Thomas Jett and William Bernard a parcel of land situate in the Parish of Washington and County aforesaid containing 400 acres which the said Francis Williams and purchased in fee from the Rev. Joseph Simpson in trust to be sold for the payment of his the said Francis Williams debts and whereas the said Thomas Jett and William Bernard in pursuance of the said trust have executed to the said Charles Morris an indenture of bargain and sale for the legal and absolute conveyance of the said tract of land to the said Charles Morris the consideration therein mentioned; but whereas the said Charles Morris hath judged it necessary for a further confirmation of this title therein also to take a conveyance for the same with general warranty from the said Francis Williams these presents witnesseth that the said Francis Williams as well for in consideration of the sum of 130 pounds by the said Charles Morris paid to the said Thomas Jett and William Bernard as trustees for the purposes aforesaid as for and in consideration of the sum of five shillings also by the said Charles Morris to the said Francis Williams in hand paid the receipt of which the said Francis doth hereby acknowledge is granted bargained and sold by these presents unto the said Charles Morris forever all his right title interest property claim and demand whatsoever to the said tract of land and premises with the appurtenances thereof. In witness whereof the said Francis Williams and Mary Williams his wife have hereunto set their hands and seals the day and year above written.
Signed sealed and delivered in presence of Francis Williams
John Martin
Benjamin Weeks
William Bernard
At a court held for Westmoreland County the 29th day of August 1769 this indenture and the receipt annexed were acknowledged by Francis Williams party thereto and ordered to be recorded. Teste

Page 34.
Bernard to Morris
Whereas William Bernard and Thomas Jett as trustees for Francis Williams and the said Francis Williams himself by their several indentures of bargain and sale the said William Bernard and Thomas Jett, with special and the said Francis Williams with general warranty had conveyed to Charles Morris a certain piece of land in the said indenture specified for the consideration therein expressed and whereas also Mary Williams his wife of the said Francis Williams being entitled to dower in the said tract of land and refusing to join in the said conveyance and to release her dower therein; witness that the said William Bernard in consideration of the purchase money mentioned in the before recited deed paid to him by the said Charles Morris and for and in consideration of a collateral security given by the said Francis Williams to the said William Bernard he the said William Bernard doth undertake and promise to indemnify the said Charles Morris against any claim or demand of dower that the said Mary Williams may or can set up in the said tract of land in case she should survive the said Francis her husband. In witness whereof the said William Bernard have hereunto set his hand and seal this [blank] day of [blank] 1769.
In presence of William Bernard
At a court held for Westmoreland County the 29th day of August 1769 this deed was acknowledged by William Bernard party thereto and ordered to be recorded. Teste

Page 34.
Pratt & Bunbury to Edrington Indenture
This indenture made the 28th day of August 1769 between Margaret Pratt and Thomas

Bunbury acting executors of Thomas Pratt, deceased of the one part and Daniel Edrington of the Parish of Washington in County of Westmoreland of the other part. Whereas the said Thomas Pratt late of the County of Stafford by his last will and testament duly proved and recorded in the County Court of Stafford did among other things give and devise to his son Thomas Pratt and to his heirs the following pieces of land, to wit; the tract of land whereon his sister Hungerford lived in the County of King George, the tract known by the name of the Forest Quarter, and the tract called Chapman's, but directed and in his said will did authorize his executors to sell and dispose of the said land called Chapman's and to make effectual conveyances in the law for the same if they could dispose of it for such a price as they should think equal to its value, but if not in such case, he confirmed the devise of the same to his son Thomas Pratt and of his said will did constitute and appoint the said Margaret Pratt, as long as she should remain a widow, Robert Brooking, Vivion Brooking and the said Thomas Bunbury executors as by the said will; and whereas the said Margaret Pratt still containing sole and the said Thomas Bunbury having alone taken upon themselves of burthen of the execution of the said will and having been offered by the said Daniel Edrington for the said tract of land called Chapman's the sum of 200 pounds current money which was the best price that could be got for the same in which the said Margaret Pratt and Thomas Bunbury believed to be the full value thereof. This indenture therefore witnesseth that the said Margaret Pratt and Thomas Bunbury for and in consideration of 200 pounds have sold by these presents to Daniel Edrington the said tract of land called Chapman's containing 300 acres or thereabouts and bounded upon the line of John Price's land from a post upon the main road and along the said line to the dam one of the head branches of Upper Machodoc, thence along the said dam to the land of Charles Stuart, and along his line to the main road crossing the same to the old line and from thence to the beginning. In witness whereof the said Margaret Pratt and Thomas Bunbury have hereunto set their hands and seals the day and year above written.

Signed sealed and delivered in presence of — Margaret Pratt
James Dishman, Copland Pierce — Thomas Bunbury
Nicholas Muse, Elizabeth Pratt

At a court held for Westmoreland County the 29th day of August 1769 this indenture and the receipt underwritten were proved by the oaths of James Dishman, Copland Pierce and Nicholas Muse witnesses thereto and ordered to be recorded. Teste

Page 37.
Smith to Smith

I Peter Smith, Sr., The Parish of Cople and County of Westmoreland and the colony of Virginia for the natural love and affection which I have and do bear towards my loving son Peter Smith, Jr., of the Parish and County aforesaid do give by these presents 60 acres of land in the following bounds it being the land whereon my son Peter Smith now lives and part of a parcel of land formerly purchased of George Searle; viz, beginning on the land of Hon. Robert Carter, Esq. and binding on the land of Mr. Frances Wright, Mrs. Elizabeth McFarlane and Capt. Benedict Middleton, and the branch and valley to be the division between the said land given my son Peter Smith and the land where on I now live. In witness whereof to these presents I have hereunto set my hand and seal this 29th day of July 1769.

Signed sealed and delivered in the presence of — Peter Smith
James Baley, William Smith
Haraway Jackson (his mark)

At a court held for Westmoreland County the 29th day of August 1769 this indenture was proved by the oaths of James Baley, William Smith and Haraway Jackson the witnesses thereto and ordered to be recorded. Teste

Page 38.
Campbell to Boyd Mortgage

This indenture made the first day of March 1769 between Gilbert Campbell of the County of Westmoreland of the one part and David Boyd of the County of Northumberland of the other part. Witnesseth that Gilbert Campbell in consideration of 69 pounds current money of Virginia has sold to David Boyd two Slaves; Robin and Tom. To have and to hold the said slaves unto David Boyd, and form following, to wit, that he the said Gilbert Campbell now is the absolute owner of the said slaves and that he the said Gilbert Campbell will warrant and defend against all other persons and the said Gilbert Campbell will well and truly pay to the said David Boyd the sum of 69 pounds on or before the eighth day of May next together with lawful interest at the rate of 5% per annum, provided nevertheless that if the said Gilbert Campbell shall well and truly pay or cause to pay to the said David Boyd on or before the eighth day of May next ensuing the date of these presents and keep indemnified the said David Boyd against a bond entered into by the said Gilbert Campbell and David Boyd as security for the said Gilbert Campbell to Archibald McCall, then the said indenture of bargain and sale and every clause thereof to be from henceforward utterly void and of no effect. In witness whereof the said parties to these presents have hereunto set their hands and seals the day and year above written.

Sealed and delivered in the presence of. — Gilbert Campbell
Reuben Jordan — David Boyd

At a court held for Westmoreland County the 29th day of August 1769 this indenture of mortgage was proved by the oath of Reuben Jordan the witness thereto and ordered to be recorded. Teste

Page 39.
Orr & Wife to Bridges Lease

This indenture made the 22nd day of August 1769 between John Orr and Susanna Orr his wife of the Parish of Hanover and County of King George of the one part and William Bridges of the Parish of Brunswick and County of King George of the other part. Witnesseth that John Orr and Susanna Orr his wife in consideration of five shillings has sold unto William Bridges a tract of land containing 65 acres from the day next before the day of the date of these presents and the full term of one whole year yielding and paying the rent of one ear of Indian corn before the feast of Saint Michael the Archangel to the intent and purpose that by virtue of these presents and of the statute for transferring uses into possession the said William Bridges may be in actual possession of the said premises and to be better enabled to accept and take a grant and release of the reversion and inheritance thereof; and bounded as follows; beginning at a red oak standing on a branch, thence running on Nathaniel Butler's lines to a red oak by the road side, thence running to a white oak by the horse path, thence up the said line of Lawrence Butler to the head of Rappahannock, thence up the said branch to an oak and a gum marked in a branch of the said swamp, thence to a marked red oak standing by the roadside and to a marked chestnut standing at the head of the aforesaid branch, thence to the beginning. It being part of a greater tract of land which Christopher Butler, deceased, [devised] amongst his sons. In witness whereof the said John Orr and Susanna Orr his wife hath to this present indenture set their hands and seals the day month and year first above written.

Sealed and delivered in presence of — John Orr
Thomas Jett, William Strother — Susanna Orr
Charles Deane, Nicholas Muse
James Thomas

Page 41.
Orr & Wife Release to Bridges

This indenture made the 23rd day of August 1769 between John Orr and Susanna Orr his wife of the Parish of Hanover and County of King George of the one part and William Bridges of the Parish of Brunswick and County of King George of the other part. Witnesseth that John

Orr and Susanna Orr his wife in consideration of pounds current money has released unto William Bridges in his actual possession, by virtue of a bargain and sale bearing date the day next before the date of the date of these presents for the term of one whole year by force of the statute for transferring uses into possession a tract of land containing 65 acres and bounded as follows; beginning at a red oak standing on a branch, thence running on Nathaniel Butler's lines to a red oak by the road side, thence running to a white oak by the horse path, thence up the said line of Lawrence Butler to the head of Rappahannock, thence up the said branch to an oak and a gum marked in a branch of the said swamp, thence to a marked red oak standing by the roadside and to a marked chestnut standing at the head of the aforesaid branch, thence to the beginning. It being part of a greater tract of land which Christopher Butler, deceased, devised amongst his sons. In witness whereof the parties have hereunto set their hands and seals the day month and year first above written.

Sealed and delivered in presence of — John Orr
Thomas Jett, — Susanna Orr
William Strother
Charles Deane, Nicholas Muse
James Thomas

To John Triplett, Thomas Jett and William Robinson of the County of King George, Gent. Whereas John Orr and Susanna Orr his wife by their indenture of lease and release bearing date respectfully the 22nd and 23rd days of August 1769 have sold and conveyed unto William Bridges the fee simple estate of 65 acres of land lying in the Parish of Washington and County of Westmoreland and whereas the said Susanna cannot conveniently travel to our court to make acknowledgment. Therefore, we do give unto you or any two or more of you power to receive the acknowledgment which the said Susanna Orr shall be willing to make for you of the conveyance. Witness James Davenport, clerk of our said court the 26th day of August.

By virtue of the within commission to us directed we the subscribers personally went to Susanna Orr wife of the said John Orr and received her acknowledgment of the deeds of lease and release hereunto annexed and having examined privy and apart from her husband she there upon declared she did the same voluntarily and freely and is willing the same should be recorded in the County Court of Westmorland all of which we certified under our hands and seals this 26th day of August 1769.

Thomas Jett
William Robinson

At a court held for Westmoreland County the 29th day of August 1769 these indentures of lease and release and the receipt on the said release endorsed were proved by the oaths of William Strother, Charles Deane and James Thomas witnesses thereto and together with a commission annexed for taking the acknowledgment and privy examination of Susanna Orr the wife of John Orr party thereto and a certificate of the execution thereof ordered to be recorded. Teste

Page 45.

<u>Moxley to Sanford Indenture Tripartite</u>

This indenture tripartite May 29 day of August 1769 between John Moxley of the Parish of Washington and County of Westmoreland, planter of the first part, Barbary Moxley, Eleanor Moxley, Augustine Moxley, Jemima Moxley, Mary Moxley, Jr., John Moxley, Jr., James Moxley, and Sarah Moxley, children of the said John Moxley and Barbary Walker, granddaughter of the said John of the second part and Robert Sanford of the said county of the third part. Witnesseth that John Moxley in consideration of the natural love and affection which he bears to his said children as for the sum of five shillings paid by the said Robert Sanford has sold unto the said Robert Sanford all that tract of land whereon the said John Moxley lived called the Home Plantation lying in the parish and county aforesaid; and also the following estate, to wit: seven Negroes; Beck, Winney, Will, Suckey, Sarah, Asom, Frank and Daniel, one roan horse, one choice cow and calf, one sow and pigs, one bed and furniture, and one ewe and sows, and all other the estate of the said John Moxley except his wearing apparel. To have and to hold the said tract of land with all and singular the premises therein unto the said Robert Sanford to the uses intents and purposes following, to wit; To the use of the said John Moxley for and during his natural life and after his decease,

Negro Beck to the use of Barbary Moxley and her heirs in full of every part of the said John Moxley's estate.

Negro Winney to the use of Eleanor Moxley and her heirs in full of every part of the said John Moxley's estate.

Negroe Will, one roan horse, one choice cow and calf, one sow and pigs, one bed and furniture, one ewe and sows, to the use of the said Augustine Moxley and his heirs forever in full of every part of the said John Moxley's estate.

Negro Suckey to the use of Jemima Moxley and her heirs in full of every part of the said John Moxley's estate.

Negro Sarah to the use of Mary Moxley, Jr., and her heirs in full of every part of the said John Moxley's estate.

Negro man Asom to the use of John Moxley, Jr., and his heirs in full of every part of the said John Moxley's estate

Negro boy Frank to the use of Jane Moxley and her heirs in full of every part of the said John Moxley's estate.

Negro boy Daniel to the use of Sarah Moxley and her heirs in full of every part of the said John Moxley's estate.

And 50 pounds to the use of the said Barbary Walker upon condition that she nor any person claims under pretense of a promise made by the said John Moxley to his mother or father any further sum from his estate.

Lastly, the rest and residue of the said premises to the use of such person or persons as the said John Moxley, the father by any deed in writing or by his last will and testament shall appoint or direct. In witness whereof the parties to these presents have hereunto set their hands and seals the day and year first within written.

Sealed and delivered in the presence of us John Moxley (his mark)

At a court held for Westmoreland County the 29th day of August 1769 this indenture was acknowledged by John Moxley party thereto and ordered to be recorded

Page 47.

Jordan to Jordan Deed of Gift

This indenture made the 29th day of August 1769 between Robert Jordan of Cople Parish and County of Westmoreland of the one part and Reuben Jordan of the same Parish and County, son of the said Robert Jordan of the other part. Witnesseth that Robert Jordan in consideration of the natural love and affection which he hath and bear unto the said Reuben Jordan and for the better maintenance and livelihood of him hath given unto the said Robert Jordan all that tenement other lands situated in the said Parish of Cople and County of Westmoreland containing by estimation 100 acres which I purchased of William Carr Lane; and all that tenement of land lying in the same Parish of Cople and County of Westmoreland containing by estimation 150 acres which I purchased of Joseph Read and Barbara Read his wife, Jeffrey Johnson and Rachel Johnson his wife as by deeds of lease and release bearing date the 31st day of October 1755 and the 1st day of November 1755; together with the four following Negroes; Sillobo, Patt and her two children, James and Winney. To have and to hold the said tracts of land and Negroes only reserving my life in the last-mentioned tract of land containing 150 acres. In witness whereof I have hereunto set my hand and seal the day month and year first above written.

Signed sealed and delivered in presence of us Robert Jordan

Joseph Lane, Robert Lang

Joseph Lane, Jr.

At a court held for Westmoreland County the 29th day of August 1769 this deed of gift was proved by the oaths of Joseph Lane, Robert Lang, and Joseph Lane, Jr., witnesses thereto and ordered to be recorded. Teste

Page 48.
Hall to Hall Deed of Gift
I Leasure Hall of the Parish of Cople and County of Westmoreland for diverse good causes and valuable considerations me hereunto moving but especially for the natural love and affection which I have and do bear unto my well beloved son Jeremiah Hall have given him by these presents one tract of land taken out of the tract of Jeffries, bounded as followeth; beginning at a red oak, a line tree between Rust and Jeffries, and from thence running on the said line to a hickory, and from thence running South East to a red oak near Rust's Mill, and from thence running East to a red oak, and from thence to the red oak at the beginning. Also, I give unto my said son five Negro slaves; Harry, George, Harness, Petter, Buty together with all their increase, one bed and furniture, one desk, two chests, one box, one table, six chairs, nine pewter plates, one bason, two iron pots, one gun, one sein, one cupboard, four head of cattle, five head of sheep, two mares, one ferry oar, one canoe. In witness whereof I have hereunto set my hand and seal this fourth day of August 1769.
Signed sealed and delivered in the presence of us Leasure Hall
Vincent Rust, William Fleming
Matthew Rust, Peter Davis
At a court held for Westmoreland County the 26th day of September 1769 this deed of gift was acknowledged by Leasure Hall party thereto and ordered to be recorded. Test

Page 49.
Hall to Bailey Deed of Gift
I Leasure Hall of the Parish of Cople and County of Westmoreland for diverse good causes and valuable considerations me hereunto moving but especially for the natural love and affection which I have and do bear unto my well beloved daughter Mary Bailey and William Bailey (son in law) of the parish and county aforesaid and for the further welfare of themselves hath given by these presents during their natural lives or the longest liver of them, five Negroes; Old Frank, Young Frank, Let daughter of Frank, Sam and Glasgow and their increase and after their decease to be divided amongst their heirs and for the want of such heirs the Negroes to be returned and equally divided between my son Jeremiah Hall and my daughter Ann Lewis. In witness whereof I have hereunto set my hand and seal this 4th day of August 1769.
Signed sealed and delivered in the presence of us Leasure Hall
Vincent Rust, William Fleming
Matthew Rust, Peter Davis
At a court held for Westmoreland County the 26th day of September 1769 this deed of gift was acknowledged by Leasure Hall party thereto and ordered to be recorded. Test

Page 50.
Monroe Executor of Whiting to McCarty Indenture
This indenture made the 26th day of September 1769 between Andrew Monroe only acting executor of Thomas Whiting, deceased and Daniel McCarty. Whereas the said Thomas Whiting by his last will and testament duly proved and recorded, directed that the tract of land whereon he lived situate in the Parish of Washington and County of Westmoreland upon Monroe's Creek in the Irish Neck should remain unsold until his daughter Lizey Whiting was married or arrived to the age of 18 years at which time he directed the said tract of land to be sold and the money arising thence to be equally divided among his four children, and whereas Andrew Monroe having alone take upon himself the burthen and execution of the said will did after Lizey arrived to the age of 18 years, did expose to sale to the highest

bidder the said tract of land, and the said Daniel McCarty having offered for the same 152 pounds which was the most money that could be got. This indenture therefore witnesseth that Andrew Monroe in consideration of the said sum of money doth sell unto the said Daniel McCarty the said tract containing by estimation 105 acres. In witness whereof the said Andrew Monroe hath hereunto set his hand and seal the day and year first above written.
Signed sealed and delivered in presence of Andrew Monroe
At a court held for Westmoreland County the 26th day of September 1769, this indenture of bargain and sale and the receipt endorsed were acknowledged by Andrew Monroe acting executor of Thomas Whiting, deceased, and ordered to be recorded. Teste

Page 51.
William Grace's Will
In the name of God, Amen, The 26th day of September 1769, I William Grace of the County of Westmoreland being in perfect sense and memory do make and ordain this my last will and testament in manner and form following.
Item I give and bequeath to my loving wife Ann Grace for and during her natural life, Negro man Dick, Negro woman Doll and Negro boy Billy.
Item as to son Thomas Grace I give two pounds sterling money
As likewise my daughter Ann Bell I give one shilling sterling.
Item I give and bequeath to my son John Grace half my land in North Carolina being 172 acres and after the death of his mother, Negro boy Billy, and in case the said John should die without heirs, I entail the said negroes and their increase to my son James Grace.
Item I give and bequeath to my son William Grace 65 pounds current money to be paid by my executor James Grace.
Item I give and bequeath to my son James Grace, Negro boys Bristol and James, and Negro girl Hannah, and after the decease of his mother, Negro Dick. I likewise give him a young man called Jewell and two thirds of the residue of all my moveable estate and do hereby appoint him to be my sole executor of this my last will and testament. In witness whereof I have hereunto set my hand and fixed my seal the day and month and year first written.
Signed sealed and delivered in presence of William Grace
Presley Hall, John Pillian (his mark)
Richard Lowe
At a court held for Westmoreland County the 28th day of November 1769, this will was proved according to law by the oaths of John Pillian and Richard Lowe witnesses thereto and ordered to be recorded and on the motion of James Grace the executor therein named who made oath thereto according to law and together with William Baley and Richard Lowe his securities entered into and acknowledged bond with condition as the law directs, certificate is granted him for obtaining a probate thereof in due form. Test.

Page 53.
Francis Callis' Will
I Francis Callis of Cople Parish and County of Westmoreland do make this my last will and testament in manner and form as follows.
All my land in Fauquier County I desire may be sold by my executors and the money equally divided amongst my children.
I give to my brother Robert Callis 10 pounds current money.
I give all the residue of my estate both real and personal to my loving wife, Jane Callis for and during her natural life in order to enable her the better to bring up, support, and educate my children in the best manner the estate will afford until they arrive to the age of 21 years or are married, then as they come of age or are married as aforesaid shall then have an equal part of my estate for, always having in reserve, one third part of my estate for the support of my wife. But if my wife should marry, in that case I order that she may have only a third part

of my estate and the remainder to be equally divided amongst my children.
I constitute and appoint my wife Jane Callis executrix [and] my good friends, Fleet Cox, Francis Wright, Richard Callis, Ambrose Callis and Thomas Callis, executors of this my last will and testament. In witness whereof I have hereunto set my hand and seal this 6th September 1769.
Signed, sealed and acknowledged in the presence of Francis Callis
Elizabeth McFarlane
John Redman
William B. Flood
At a court held for Westmoreland County the 27th day of February this will was proved according to law by the oaths of Elizabeth McFarlane, John Redman and William Flood, the witnesses thereto and ordered to be recorded. And on the motion of Jane Callis, Fleet Cox and Francis Wright three of the executors therein named who made oath thereto according to law and together with the said William Flood their security entered into and acknowledged bond with condition as the law directs certificate is granted them for obtaining a probate thereof in due form; liberty being reserved to the other executors therein named to join in the probate thereof when they should think fit. Teste

Page 54.
Sarah Ellen Middleton's Will
In the name of God, Amen, I Sarah Ellen Middleton of the Parish of Cople and the County of Westmoreland, being sick and weak of body, but of sound and perfect memory do make this my last will and testament in manner and form following.
Item my will and desire is that whatsoever estate I have, or bequeathed to me by my deceased husband be ordered and disposed of according to his directions in his last will and testament.
Lastly, I appoint my trusty friends, Mr. Fleet Cox, Francis Wright and Daniel Bennett my executors of this my last will and testament. In witness whereof, I the said Sarah Ellen Middleton have hereunto set my hand and seal this 23rd day of July 1769.
Signed sealed and delivered in presence of Sarah Ellen Middleton (her mark)
James Baley
Betty Proctor
At a court held for Westmoreland County the 27th day of February 1770 this will was proved according to law by the oaths of James Baley and Betty Proctor. The witnesses thereto and ordered to be recorded. And on the motion of Francis Wright and Daniel Bennett two of the executors therein named who made oath thereto according to law and together with William Flood and William Rice their securities, entered into, and acknowledged bond with condition as the law directs, certificate is granted them for obtaining a probate thereof in due form.
Memorandum, Fleet Cox the other executor in the said will named personally appeared and refused to take upon himself the burthen of the execution thereof. Teste

Page 55.
Butler & Wife to Rice
This indenture made the 3rd day of May 1769 between William Butler and Rebecca Butler his wife of Cople Parish and County of Westmoreland, planter of the one part and William Rice of the same parish and county, planter of the other part. Witnesseth that William Butler and Rebecca Butler his wife in consideration of 76 pounds, 2 shillings and 6 pence current money of Virginia have sold unto William Rice all that tract lying in Yeocomico Neck and the Parish of Cople and County of Westmoreland containing 43 ½ acres and bounded as followeth; beginning at a large white oak corner with Thomas Butler, Sr., and running along a crooked line of marked trees South 75° West 11 pole, South 86 ¼ ° West 24 pole, North 82° West 9 pole, North 74 ¼ ° West 20 pole to a pine tree corner with Thomas Butler, thence North 8 ½ ° West 8 pole, thence North 12° East 4 pole, thence North 12° West18 pole, thence North 22

¼ ° West 18 pole to a poplar, another corner to Thomas Butler, Sr., thence South 77° West to the creek, thence up the said creek and a branch to a large mulberry tree, thence South 44 ½ ° East to the beginning. The same being a tract of land conveyed by Thomas Butler, Sr., to the said William Butler in fee by deeds bearing date [blank]. In witness whereof the first parties to these presents have interchangeably set their hands and seals the day and year first above written.

Signed sealed and delivered in the presence of
Richard Halliday
George Halliday
Stephen Self, Sr. (his mark)

William Butler
Rebecca Butler (her mark)

At a court held for Westmoreland County the 27th day of February 1770 this indenture of feoffment together with the memorandum of livery of seizen and receipt endorsed were acknowledged by William Butler and Rebecca Butler his wife parties thereto (she being first privy examined as the law directs) and ordered to be recorded. Teste

Page 57.
Robinson to Hutt Indenture
This indenture made the 6th of March 1770 between William Robinson and his son John Robinson and Easter Robinson his wife of the Parish of Cople and County of Westmoreland, planter of the one part and Gerard Hutt of the aforesaid parish and county of the other part. Witnesseth that William Robinson and John Robinson and Easter Robinson his wife in consideration of 120 pounds current money has sold unto Gerard Hutt all that plantation and tract of land containing 170 acres being in the Parish of Cople and County of Westmoreland, the land whereon Thomas Robinson formerly lived on now vested lawfully in the said William Robinson and John Robinson and his wife adjoining to the land of Landon Carter's called Panticoe and the lands of John Crabb's. In witness whereof the said parties first above mentioned to these presents have interchangeably set their hands and seals the day and year above written.

Signed sealed and delivered in presence of us
Gerard Hutt, Jr.
William Brown
George McKenney

William Robinson (his mark)
John Robinson
Easter Robinsoni (her mark)

At a court held for Westmoreland County the 24th day of April 1770 this indenture was acknowledged by William Robinson and John Robinson and Easter Robinson his wife parties thereto, the said Easter being first privy examined as the law directs and ordered to be recorded. Teste

Page 59.
Robins & Wife to Stuart [Steward] Indenture
This indenture made the 11th day of January 1770 between Thomas Robins and Sarah Robins his wife of the County of Westmoreland of the one part and Jeremiah Stuart of the County of King George of the other part. Witnesseth that Thomas Robins and Sarah Robins his wife in consideration of 100 pounds current money of Virginia has sold unto Jeremiah Stuart all that tract ling and being for the most part in the County of Westmoreland, a small part thereof extending into the County of King George, containing by estimation 200 acres which said plantation descended to the said Thomas Robins at the death of his father Thomas Robins who purchased the said plantation of one Francis Wright by whose deed the title and bounds may more particular appear. At this present time the said plantation and land is adjacent to and surrounded by the lands of George Riding, the Glebe land of Washington Parish and that of Moses Pitman. In witness whereof the said Thomas Robins and Sarah Robins have hereunto set their hands and seals the day and year above written.

Signed sealed and delivered in presence of
Samuel Oldham, Peter Jett

Thomas Robins
Sarah Robins

Benjamin Stuart, James Stuart
To Samuel Oldham, and Archibald Campbell, Gent. Whereas Thomas Robins and Sarah Robins his wife by their indenture of bargain and sale bearing date the 11th day of January 1770 have sold unto Jeremiah Stuart the fee simple estate of 200 acres lying in the Parish of Washington and County of Westmoreland and whereas the said Sarah Robins cannot conveniently travel to our court of Westmoreland to make acknowledgement. Therefore, we do give unto you or any two of you power to receive the acknowledgement which the said Sarah Robins shall be willing to make. Witness, James Davenport, clerk of our said court the 10th day of January 1770.
West. Sct. We the subscribers in obedience to the above writ went to Sarah Robins and examined her privy and apart from her husband concerning conveyance hereunto annexed and do hereby certify that she did declare to us that she doth freely and voluntarily acknowledge the conveyance and she is willing the same be recorded in the court of Westmoreland County. Given under our hands and seals this 11th day of January 1770.
Samuel Oldham
Archibald Campbell
At a court held for Westmoreland County the 26th day of June 1770, this indenture and the receipt endorsed were proved by the oaths of Peter Jett, Benjamin Stuart and James Stuart, witnesses thereto and together with the commission annexed for taking the acknowledgement and privy examination of Sarah Robins wife of Thomas Robins and a certificate of the execution thereof ordered to be recorded.

Page 62.
Pierce & Wife to Massey Release
This indenture made the 17th day of March 1770 between Copeland Pierce and Ann Pierce his wife of the Parish of Washington and County of Westmoreland of the one part and of the parish and county aforesaid the other part. Witnesseth that Copeland Pierce and Ann Pierce his wife in consideration of 220 pounds current money of Virginia doth sell and release to Robert Massey in his actual possession all that tract of land lying in the Parish of Washington and County of Westmoreland containing 200 acres. Which said tract of land was purchased by the said Copeland Pierce from Robert Massey and conveyed by a deed of sale which deed was duly proved and recorded [28th day of July 1767]. In witness whereof the said Copeland Pierce and Ann Pierce his wife have hereunto interchangeably set their hands and seals the day month and year first above written.
Sealed and delivered in presence of us — Copeland Pierce
Daniel Edrington, Lovell Bryan — Ann Pierce
John Weedon, Mary Edrington
At a court held for Westmoreland County the 26th day of June 1770 this indenture and receipt endorsed were acknowledged by Copeland Pierce and Ann Pierce his wife parties thereto she being first privy examined as the law directs and ordered to be recorded. Teste

Page 63.
Bradley Garner's Will
In the name of God, Amen.
Item I leave my executors to have the use of all my Negroes, but Connon, for four years to raise money to pay debts with.
Item I give my son George Garner 95 acres of land my father left me by deed of gift and 120 acres of land I bought of Samuel Garner after his mother's decease and Negroes Harry and Luce.
Item I leave my sons George Garner and Vincent Garner 210 acres of land I bought of William Spite in North Carolina where William Harden now lives and Negroes Tom and Will.
Item I leave my daughter Eleanor Garner, Negro wench Eady in trust after her mother Catherine Garner's decease and for want of heirs to my daughter Lettice Garner.

Item I leave my daughter Hannah Cox, Negro wench Phillish.
Item I leave my daughter Elizabeth Garner, Negro Winni. And for want of heirs to be equally divided between my three sons Benjamin Garner, George Garner and Vincent Garner.
Item I leave my daughter Lettice Garner, Negro Jean and for want of heirs to my three aforesaid sons to be equally divided.
I leave these courses and lines to be the bounds between Francis Garner and my two sons Benjamin Garner and Vincent Garner and she beginning near a white oak thence South 51° East along a line of marked trees to where there stood a pine near the place where John Trammell formerly lived, thence North 51° East 20 poles to a branch and down the branch and marsh and pond to a marked pine and across the pond South by West 20 pole to a cedar on the beach of sand at Potomack River, side.
Item I give my son Benjamin Garner about 100 acres of land as I bought of Richard Lee, Esq. in Ragged Point Neck, beginning at a red oak corner to Mr. John Crabb of and Robert Middleton, thence along a line of marked trees to the back line of Hurd's patent South by West near to a white oak corner with Francis Garner's, thence cross the branch to a mulberry tree near where John Trammell formerly lived, thence straight crossed the old field to a persimmon tree in Joseph Garner's lease, thence along the bounds of the lease to a cove to the beginning including the house where he now lives; and Negro Connon.
Item I give my son Vincent Garner all the remainder part of that land I bought of Richard Lee, Esq. in Ragged Point Neck, and Negro Ben and for want of heirs the land to my son Benjamin Garner and the Negro to my son George Garner.
Item I give my grandson Thomas Pritchett, Negro girl Frank, as I allotted his mother and her increase to him and his heirs, he paying his sister Catharine Pritchett half the value of her at the age of 18 years.
Item I leave Rodham Pritchett one silver watch as he has in his possession.
Item I leave the 632 acres of land I bought of John Jarvis to be sold by order of my executors and one Negro called Jim to raise money to pay my debts with.
Item I give my loving wife Catherine Garner the use of Negroes Jean and Mereon, and half of the rest of my estate after my just debts are paid, for natural life and then to be equally divided between my four sons and three daughters namely Benjamin Garner, George Garner, Jeremiah Garner, Vincent Garner, Eleanor Garner, Letty Garner and Elizabeth Garner and their heirs forever.
Lastly, I make and ordain constitute and appoint my loving wife Catherine Garner and my son Benjamin Garner and Peter Cox executrix and executors of this my last will and testament. In witness whereof I have hereunto set my hand and seal this 13th day of October 1769.
Signed sealed and acknowledge in the presence of us Bradley Garner
Presley Hall, Ashton Hall
John Grace
codicil;
I give my son Benjamin Garner 100 acres of land I bought of Arther Cuck [Arthur Cox?].
Item I give my son Vincent Garner 100 acres of land I bought of Nicholas Noil where John Bradley formerly lived.
Item I leave my daughter Elizabeth Garner 50 acres of land I bought of Nicholas Noil where James Polly formerly lived.
Item I give Frances Garner daughter of Abraham Garner, deceased 50 acres of land I bought of Thomas Horn in North Carolina.
Item I leave my daughter Hannah Cox one cow and calf and the two Negroes I left my son George Garner she is to have when he arrives at 21 years old and the value of five years before of this work.
I give my son Vincent Garner, Negro James.
Bradley Garner
At a court held for Westmoreland County the 26th day of June 1770 this will was presented in court by Peter Cox one of the executors therein named and motion been made that the heir

at law should be summonsed to contest the probate of the said will he personally appeared in court and consented to the probate thereof and therefore the same was proved according to law by the oaths of Presley Hall and Ashton Hall witnesses thereto and the codicil underwritten not been witnessed, the same were proved to be the proper hand writing of the testator by the oaths of the said Presley Hall and Ashton Hall and together with the said will are ordered to be recorded and on the motion of the said Peter Cox who made oath thereto according to law and together with Thomas Fisher and Charles Bennett his securities entered into and acknowledged bond with condition as the law directs, certificate is granted him for obtaining a probate thereof in due form. Teste

Page 66.
Harrison & Wife to Ballantine & Company Mortgage
This indenture made this fifth day of December 1769 between John Harrison and Elizabeth Harrison his wife of the Parish of Cople and County of Westmoreland of the one part and James Ballantine and Company, merchants of Glasgow of the other part. Witnesseth that John Harrison and Elizabeth Harrison his wife in consideration of 20 pounds current money of Virginia has sold unto James Ballantine and Company all that tract of land whereon we now live containing 130 acres bounded as followeth; beginning at a small chestnut in the line of George Harrison and running thence South 48° East 134 poles to a swamp running into Smith's Mill Pond, thence down the said swamp North 39° East 93 poles, thence North 5° West 32 poles, thence North 25° East 56 poles to the land of Frances Wright, thence North 76° West 156 poles to a red oak corner tree to the land of George Harrison, and thence South 12° West 109 poles to the first beginning. Provided nevertheless that if we the said John Harrison and Elizabeth Harrison his wife do well and truly pay unto the said James Ballantine and Company the said sum of 20 pounds current money of Virginia with legal interest thereon before the 10th day of December next ensuing in this instrument of writing and the sale hereby made to be void and of none effect. In witness whereof we have hereunto set our hands and seals the day and year above written.

Signed sealed and delivered in presence of
Charles Bennett
William Harrison
Hugh Hamilton
Patrick Ballantine

John Harrison (his mark)
Elizabeth Harrison (her mark)

County, Virginia Deeds & Wills 1768-1773; DB-15 {Abstract by Mike Marshall}; Page 68.
Tebbs & Wife to Ballantine Mortgage
This indenture made the ninth day of December 1769 between Daniel Tebbs of Cople Parish and County of Westmoreland and Elizabeth Tebbs his wife of the one part and John Ballantine of said parish and county of the other part. Witnesseth that Daniel Tebbs in consideration of 524 pounds, 15 shillings current money of Virginia has sold unto John Ballantine a tract of land lying in the said parish and county near Yeocomico Church being part of a tract given to the said Daniel Tebbs by the last will of his father Daniel Tebbs, deceased and is bounded as followeth; beginning at a stake by the road that leads to Yeocomico Warehouse, corner with William Tebbs, thence South 36° West 58 poles to a stake in a line of Samuel Rust, North 53° West 100 poles to another stake, thence North 31 degrees 30 minutes West 69 poles to a scrub by hickory, thence South 31° West 141 poles to a chestnut tree, North 63° 45 minutes West 57 poles to a stake supposed to be a corner with the Hon. Thomas Lord Fairfax, thence North 27° West 210 poles to a small white oak blazed on Rotank Branch, thence down the said branch the several meanders, thereof to a stake near the mill dam, thence southeast 75 poles to a large cedar tree by the roadside, thence South 11° East 92 poles to another stake by the said roadside, thence along the said road to the beginning containing 466 acres. In witness whereof the parties to these presents Interchangeably set their hands and seals the day and year first above written.

Signed sealed and delivered in the presence of Daniel Tebbs
Thomas Fisher, Joseph Garner (his mark) Elizabeth Tebbs
John Meals, Samuel Rust (his mark)
At a court held for Westmoreland County the 26th day of June 1770 this indenture and the receipt endorsed were proved by the oaths of John Meals and Samuel Rust witnesses thereto and the same having been before proved by the oath of Thomas Fisher one other of the witnesses thereto are ordered to be recorded. Test

Page 71.
McCarty & Wife to Rust
This indenture made the 25th day of February 1768 between Daniel McCarty of the Parish of Washington and County of Westmoreland and Winifred McCarty his wife of the other part and Jeremiah Rust of the said county and Parish of Cople of the other part. Witnesseth that Daniel McCarty and Winifred McCarty his wife in consideration of 50 pounds current money of Virginia has sold unto Jeremiah Rust all that tract of land in the Parish of Cople and County of Westmoreland containing 50 acres bounded as followeth; beginning at Yeocomico River to a cove called the Old Warehouse Cove, and up the said cove to the head, thence along the land of Jeremiah Bailey to Mullins Cove, from thence down the said cove to Yeocomico Creek and then to Yeocomico River to the beginning. In witness whereof the parties to these presents have hereunto set their hands and seals the day and year above written.
Sealed and delivered in presence of Daniel McCarty
Charles Weeks, Elizabeth Gordon Winifred McCarty
Elizabeth McCall
At a court held for Westmoreland County the 26th day of June 1770 this indenture was acknowledged by Daniel McCarty and Winifred McCarty his wife parties thereto and the receipt endorsed was also acknowledged by the said Daniel and together with the said indenture ordered to be recorded. Teste

Page 72.
John Atwell's Will
In the name of God, Amen, the seventh day of April 1770, I John Atwell of the County of Westmoreland being very sick and weak of body but perfect mind and memory do make and ordain this my last will and testament.
Item I give and bequeath to my son Thomas Atwell all my lands whereon I now live on the side of Machodoc Creek to him and his heirs and for want of such heirs to my son John Atwell and for want of such heirs to my son Richard Atwell.
Item I give and bequeath to my son Francis Atwell all my lands purchased of Thomas Riddell lying in Machodoc Neck to him and his heirs and for want of such heirs to my son John Atwell and for want of heirs of him to my son Richard Atwell.
Item I give and bequeath to my son Thomas Atwell, old Negro woman Nan.
Item I give my daughter Elizabeth Lafon, three Negroes; Tom, Oringe and Belinda, and no more of my estate than what she has already had.
I give to my daughter Sarah Coghill, Negro girl Peg, Negro boy Nat, and six breeding ewes and no more of my estate than what she has already had.
Item I give to my brother Francis Atwell, 5 pounds to be laid out in a suit of clothes by my executors.
Item I give and bequeath all my Negroes and all other estate not before given to be equally divided between my children, namely, Thomas Atwell, John Atwell, Francis Atwell, Richard Atwell, Youell Atwell, Ann [Sarah] Coghill, Martha Atwell and William Atwell to them and their heirs.
It is my will and desire that my brother Francis Atwell shall live on the place he now lives during his life and that he should have liberty of firewood and as much corn ground as he or

one hand can tend, and that he shall make 20 pair of shoes per year for rent to be paid to my executors for the use of my estate. It is my will and desire my daughter Martha Atwell shall live with my son Thomas Atwell until she arrives at the year of 21 or day of marriage and that she shall not marry or make any contract of marriage without the consent of her three brothers, Thomas Atwell, John Atwell and Richard Atwell. It is my desire that my son Thomas Atwell shall keep her estate for her so she arrives at the age of 21 or day of marriage.
It is my will and desire that my son William Atwell be found good working clothes out of my estate during his apprenticeship.
It is my desire my Negroes be kept together to make and finish this crop.
I constitute, make and ordain my sons Thomas Atwell, John Atwell and Richard Atwell my soul executors of this my last will and testament.
Signed sealed and declared in presence of us John Atwell
Reuben Jordan
Richard Jackson
James Sorrell
At a court held for Westmoreland County the 26th day of June 1770 this will was proved according to law by the oaths of Reuben Jordan and James Sorrell witnesses thereto and ordered to be recorded, and on the motion of Thomas Atwell and Richard Atwell two of the executors therein named who made oath thereto according to law did together with Thomas Fisher and Thomas Sorrell her securities entered into and acknowledged bond with condition as the law directs, certificate is granted them for obtaining a probate thereof in due form. Teste

Page 74.
Pendleton & Wife to Lee
This indenture made the 19th day of April 1770 between Philip Pendleton and Martha Pendleton his wife of the Parish of St. Mark and the County of Culpeper of the one part and Richard Lee, Esq. of Cople Parish and the County of Westmoreland of the other part. Witnesseth that Philip Pendleton and Martha Pendleton his wife in consideration of 300 pounds current money of Virginia has sold to Richard Lee all that tract of land lying in Machodoc Neck and the Parish of Cople and County of Westmoreland containing by estimation 200 acres adjoining to the lines of the land of William Carr Tidwell, the said Richard Lee, the heirs of William Callis, deceased, and Mary Kenner and Elizabeth Kenner, infants which said land was given by Chandler Awbrey, deceased to his son James Sorrell Awbrey who died an infant under the age of 21 years without lawful issue and then the same became vested in the said Martha Awbrey who intermarried with the said Philip Pendleton party to these presents as will appear by the last will and testament of Chandler Awbrey bearing date the ninth day of December 1755, in the following words to with, "Item I give and bequeath all my lands to my son James Sorrell Awbrey and his heirs forever but if my said son should die before he arrives at the age of 21 years without issue of his body lawfully begotten, then I give my land and plantation whereon I now live to my daughter Elizabeth Awbrey and her heirs forever; and I give my other tract of land on Machodoc River to my daughter Martha Awbrey and her heirs forever". In witness whereof the parties first above mentioned to these presents have interchangeably set their hands and seals the day and year first above written.
Signed sealed and delivered in the presence of Philip Pendleton
French Strother
William Underwood
T. Clifton
Philip Clayton, Jr.
Samuel Clayton, Jr.
To William Williams, James Slaughter, and Samuel Clayton of the County of Culpeper, Gent. Whereas Philip Pendleton and Martha Pendleton his wife by their indenture of feoffment

bearing date the 19th day of April 1770 have sold unto Richard Lee, Esq. the fee simple estate of 200 acres of land lying in the Parish of Cople and County of Westmoreland and whereas the said Martha Pendleton cannot conveniently travel to our court to make acknowledgment. Therefore, we do give unto you or any two of you power to receive the acknowledgment which the said Martha Pendleton shall be willing to make before you. Witness, James Davenport, clerk of our said court at the courthouse the 20th day of April.
Culpeper County Sct. By virtue of the within written to us directed we did personally go to the said Martha Pendleton wife of the within named Philip Pendleton and before us she did acknowledge the indenture hereunto annexed to be her act and deed and that she did the same freely and voluntarily and was willing that the same should be recorded in the County Court of Westmoreland. All which we certified to the said court under order of our hands and seals this 24th day of April 1770.
William Williams
Samuel Clayton, Jr.
At a court held for Westmoreland County the 31st day of July 1770 this indenture was proved by the oaths of French Strother, T. Clifton [Thomas Clifton], and Samuel Clayton, Jr., witnesses thereto and the memorandum of livery of seizen in receipt endorsed were also proved by the oaths of the same witnesses and together with the commission annexed for taking the acknowledgment and privy examination of Martha Pendleton and wife of Philip Pendleton party thereto and a certificate of the execution thereof ordered to be recorded. Teste

Page 79.
Graham to Flood Indenture
This indenture made the 14th day of April 1770 between John Graham and Elizabeth Graham his wife of the Parish of St. Stephen's and County of Northumberland of the one part and William Flood of the Parish of Cople and County of Westmoreland, Gent., of the other part. Whereas John Graham is seized in fee simple of a tract of land, hereinafter particularly described, which land Maj. William Taite who intermarried with the grandmother of the said John Graham, agreed in his lifetime to sell to the said William Flood for the sum of 400 pounds current money and received the consideration money, and by deed in his lifetime conveyed to the said John Graham four slaves, and by his will devised him all the residue of his estate upon condition that he the said John Graham should convey the said tract of land to the said William Flood in fee simple. Now this indenture witnesseth that in compliance with the agreement of the said William Taite, in consideration of the several donations of the said William Flood to the said John Graham and for the sum of five shillings by the said William Flood, the said John Graham and Elizabeth Graham his wife have sold unto William Flood all that tenement of land lying in the Parish of Cople and County of Westmoreland commonly called by the name of "Kinsale" containing 200 acres which said land John Graham, late of the said Parish of Cople and County of Westmoreland, merchant, deceased, died seized and possessed of having at the time of his death the said John Graham his eldest son and heir at law to whom the same descended in fee simple. In witness whereof the parties to these presents have interchangeably set their hands and seals the day and year first above written.
Signed sealed and delivered in presence of us John Graham
James Knott, Henry Lifon, Thomas Jones, Jr.
James Grant (his mark), George Knott (his mark)
Nicholas Stowers (his mark), Mary Smith (her mark)
Mary Thomas (her mark)
At a court held for Westmoreland County the 31st day of July 1770 this indenture was proved by the oaths James Knott, James Grant and Nicholas Stowers witnesses thereto and the receipt endorsed was also proved by the oath of James Knott and together with the said indenture ordered to be recorded.
John Graham's performance bond to William Flood recorded the 31st day of July 1770

Page 82.
Daniel Jackson's Will
In the name of God, Amen, I Daniel Jackson of the Parish of Cople and County of Westmoreland being in good health of body and perfect sense and memory do constitute and appoint this to be my last will and testament in manner and form following.
Item I give and bequeath to my daughter Sarah Jackson my now dwelling plantation with 50 acres of land and two Negroes; Hanner and James, and one feather bed and furniture, and if my daughters should die without heir, I give Negro James to my son William Jackson.
Item I give my son William Jackson Negro man Mott, and one feather bed.
Item my will and desire is that all the remainder part of my estate should be equally divided between my five children; George Jackson, Daniel Jackson, William Jackson, Elizabeth Franklin, and Sarah Jackson.
Item my will and desire is that my son William Jackson and my daughter Sarah Jackson the whole and sole executors of this my last will and testament. In witness whereof I have hereunto set my hand and seal the second day of May 1767.
Signed sealed and acknowledged in presence of us Daniel Jackson (his mark)
Richard Sutton
Francis Sutton, Jr.
Ann Hinson (her mark)
At a court held for Westmoreland County the 31st day of July 1770 this will was proved according to law by the oaths of Richard Sutton, Francis Sutton and Ann Hinson the witnesses thereto and ordered to be recorded, and on the motion of William Jackson and Sarah Jackson the executors therein named who made oath thereto according to law and together with John Hutt and John Robinson their securities entered into and acknowledged bond with condition as the law directs, certificate is granted them for obtaining a probate thereof in due form; previous to which, the said executors made oath that they know not whether George Jackson the heir at law of the testator be alive or where he resides. Whereupon it is ordered that the sheriff made proclamation of the probate of the said will and give notice according to law. Teste

Page 83.
Bragg & Wife to Bragg Indenture
This indenture made the 11th day of July 1770 between William Bragg and Elizabeth Bragg his wife of the Parish of Lunenburg and County of Richmond of the one part and Moore Bragg of the aforesaid Parish and County, planter of the other part. Witnesseth that William Bragg and Elizabeth Bragg his wife in consideration of 75 pounds current money of Virginia have sold unto Moore Bragg all that tract of land lying in the Parish of Cople and County of Westmoreland containing by estimation 50 acres and bounded as followeth; beginning at a small gum in Pantico Swamp, thence along a line of marked trees being the line between this land and the land of William Thomas, to a large chestnut tree corner in the said Thomas' line, thence along a line of marked trees up the said run of Pantico, a crooked line to a white oak, thence up the said run to three small chestnut tree corner to the said William Bragg and said Moore Bragg, thence to the beginning, which said land being part of a larger tract devised by Charles Bragg, deceased, father of the said William Bragg party to these presents. In witness whereof the parties first above mentioned to these presents have hereunto set their hands and seals the day and year above written.
Signed sealed and delivered in presence of William Bragg
Benjamin Brownhouse
William Robins
Griffin Garland
John Eidson
At a court held for Westmoreland County the 31st day of July 1770 this indenture of feoffment

and a memorandum of livery of seizen and receipt thereon endorsed were proved by the oath of Benjamin Brownhouse, Griffin Garland and John Eidson witnesses thereto and ordered to be recorded and Elizabeth Bragg the wife of the said William Bragg personally appeared and being first privy examined as the law directs voluntarily relinquished her right of dower in the said estate conveyed by the said indenture. Teste

Page 86.
Peirce [Pierce] & Wife to McClanahan Indenture
This indenture made the 29th day of May 1770 between Joseph Peirce, Gent of the Parish of Cople and County of Westmoreland and Sarah Elliott Peirce his wife of the one part and John McClanahan of the parish and county aforesaid of the other part. Witnesseth that Joseph Peirce and Sarah Elliott Peirce his wife in consideration of 14 shillings and six pence current money of Virginia per acre of land have sold unto John McClanahan 177 acres of land and 35 pole being a parcel in part of land formerly belonging to William Rice and Thomas Templeman, deceased lying in the aforesaid County of Westmoreland and bounded by the lands of Joseph Peirce and the land held by Mrs. Edward Ransdell, viz; beginning at a marked white oak corner to Mrs. Edward Ransdell and the said Pierce and running along a line dividing this land according to the former deed, North 58 ½°East 174 pole to a marked red oak standing near the side of the road, the same being corner tree to a parcel of land before sold out of this tract by young William Rice to Mr. Hazlerigg then along the said Hazlerigg's line South 6 ½° East 94 pole to another marked red old standing by the side of the road near the aforesaid Hazlerigg's dwelling house, thence South 35° West 80 pole to a red oak standing on a valley, thence South 37° West 40 pole to another red oak, being formerly corner tree to William Dozier and Templeton deceased, thence North 73° west 64 ½ pole to a small marked chestnut near a run, thence South 79 ½° West 14 pole to a small white oak sapling marked for a corner tree between the said Peirce and McClanahan, thence North 63° West 40 pole to a poplar marked for a corner tree between the said Peirce and McClanahan thence North 5 ¾° West 50 pole to a small gum standing near the run also marked for a corner between the said Peirce and McClanahan, thence down the said run or swamp to several meanders of the said water course to the line dividing the aforesaid land from that formerly patented by Col. Peirce, thence along that line to the first beginning.
[page 88 & 89 missing]
In witness whereof I have hereunto set our hands and fixed our seals the day and year above written.
Signed sealed and delivered in presence of — Joseph Peirce
Robert Tomlin — Sarah E. Peirce
Richard Sutton, Jr.
Edward Matthews
Hancock Lee
Received of John McClanahan the sum within mentioned which is 128 pounds, 6 shillings and 6 pence. — Joseph Peirce
Robert Tomlin — Sarah E. Peirce
Richard Sutton, Jr.
Thomas Thompson
Edward Matthews
Hancock Lee
At a court held for Westmoreland County the 31st day of July 1770 this indenture and feoffment and the memorandum of livery of seizen and receipt endorsed and proved by the oaths of Thomas Thompson, Edward Matthews, and Hancock Lee, witnesses thereto and ordered to be recorded. Teste.

Page 91.
Monroe & Wife to Kendall Indenture

This indenture made the 27th day of August 1770 between William Monroe, Jr., and Jemima Monroe his wife of the County of Westmoreland, planter of the one part and Woffendall Kendall of the said county, Sheriff of the other part. Witnesseth that William Monroe and Jemima Monroe his wife in consideration of 75 pounds current money of Virginia has sold to Woffendall Kendall, two parcels of land containing by estimation 275 ½ acres lying in the Parish of Washington and County of Westmoreland being the land that the said William Monroe purchased of James Bankhead who purchased the same lands of James Donaldson, silversmith who purchased the said lands of the assigns of William Markham who was heir to Lewis Markham to whom these two pieces of land fell by escheat.

1) The first parcel to Lewis Markham, by the death of George Thorne, as appears by the Escheat Deed from the Proprietors of the Northern Neck of Virginia bearing date the 1st day of December 1708, being 151 ½ acres bounded as followeth; Beginning at a marked red oak standing on South side of a path that leads from Mattox to Nanjatico, extending South 180 poles to the line of the land of Mr. Starke, then West 160 poles, then North to the line of William Balthrop 122 poles, finally along said Balthrop's line to the first station;

2) and the other parcel to Lewis Markham by an Escheat Deed from the Proprietors of the Northern Neck of Virginia bearing date the 7th day of December 1708 by the death of Thomas Carter, whereby the 74 acres of land is bounded as followeth; Beginning at a marked white oak close upon the Westward side of Stark's Dam extending thence North 27 ¼° West 115 poles to a corner red oak between this land and the land of Benjamin Weedon, thence North 67° East 158 poles to a red oak corner tree to the land of George Thorne standing in the line of Mr. William Balthrop, thence South 93 poles to a white oak corner tree to the land of said Thorne close upon the Dam, thence up along close upon the South side of the meanders of the dam to the first beginning. both which parcels, dividends containing together 275 ½ acres of land.

In witness whereof the said parties has hereunto set their hands and seals the day month and year written.

Sealed and delivered in the presence of — William Monroe, Jemima Monroe
John Martin
William Berryman
John Monroe
Anthony McKittrick

To William Berryman, Maj. John Martin, and Archibald Campbell, Gent. Whereas William Monroe and Jemima Monroe his wife by their indenture of bargain and sale bearing date the 27th day of August 1770 have sold unto Woffendall Kendall the fee simple estate of 275 ½ acres with the appurtenances lying in the Parish of Washington and whereas the said Jemima Monroe cannot conveniently travel to our court of Westmoreland county to make acknowledgement. Therefore, we do give unto you or any two of you power to receive the acknowledgement which the said Jemima shall be willing to make. Witness James Davenport, clerk of said court the 21st day of July 1770.

Westmoreland Sct. Agreeable to the within commission to us directed have taken the private examination of Jemima Monroe as to the passing away her right of dower and inheritance to a tract of land her husband William Monroe sold to Woffendall Kendall, who doth freely and willingly relinquished the same. Given under our hand and seals this 27th day of August 1770.
William Berryman
John Martin

At a court held for Westmoreland County the 28th day of August 1770 this indenture and the receipt endorsed were proved by the oaths of John Martin, William Berryman and Anthony McKittrick witnesses thereto and together with the commission annexed for taking the acknowledgement and privy examination of Jemima Monroe the wife of William Monroe party thereto and a certificate of the execution thereof ordered to be recorded. Teste

[boundries - refer to 1745-1747 Westmoreland County, Virginia Deeds & Will Book 10, Part 2 [Antient Press]; Page 303-306]

Page 94.
McCarty & Wife to Neale Indenture
This indenture made this [blank] day of [blank] 1770 between Daniel McCarty, Gent and Winifred McCarty his wife of the County of Westmoreland and Parish of Washington of the one part and Richard Neale of the same county and Parish of Cople of the other part. Witnesseth that Daniel McCarty and Winifred McCarty his wife in consideration of 15 pounds current money of Virginia have sold to Richard Neale all that tract in the Parish of Cople and County of Westmoreland containing 1 ¼ acres, bounded as followeth; beginning at a hickory tree and extending thence North 35° East 5 poles, thence South 33° West 22 pole, thence North 45° West 12 pole, thence North 49° East 24 pole to the beginning which said tract or parcel of land was sold and conveyed to Daniel McCarty, Sr., Lawrence Butler and Joseph Morton by Nicholas Minor by indenture bearing date the 19th day of February 1741. The same being part of a patent granted to Lord and Horton dated the 7th day of April [blank] the moiety whereof was by the said Horton sold and conveyed unto Clement Spillman and by several conveyances the same came and descended unto Nicholas Minor. In witness whereof the parties to these presents have hereunto set their hands and seals the day and year above written.
Sealed and delivered in presence of — Daniel McCarty
Presley Thornton — Winifred McCarty
Mary Griffis (her mark)
Elizabeth Thornton
At a court held for Westmoreland County the 28th day of August 1770 this indenture and the receipt endorsed were acknowledged by Daniel McCarty of party thereto and ordered to be recorded. Teste

Page 96.
Andrew Thompson's Will
In the name of God, Amen, I Andrew Thompson of Washington Parish in the County of Westmoreland being sick in body but in perfect sense and memory do make and appoint this my last will and testament in manner and form following.
Item I give to my daughter Mary Burn 20 shillings cash.
Item I desire that all my estate of what kind soever be equally divided between my son George Thompson, my son Andrew Thompson, my daughters Margaret Thompson, Sarah Thompson, Behethlem Thompson and Winifred Thompson and that my daughter Margaret Thompson's part not to be delivered to her until my son George Thompson shall arrive to the age of 21 years.
I constitute and appoint Woffendall Kendall, William Berry and John Bryan the executors of this my last will and testament. In witness whereof I have hereunto set my hand and seal this fifth day of September 1769.
Signed and sealed in presents of — Andrew Thompson (his mark)
Benjamin Settle
Thomas Rallings
James Dishman
At a court held for Westmoreland County the 28th day of August 1770 this will was proved according to law by the oath of Benjamin Settle a witness thereto and the same having been proved in November last by the oath of James Dishman another witness thereto is ordered to be recorded and on motion of Woffendall Kendall one of the executors therein named who made oath thereto according to law together with John Martin his security entered into and acknowledged bond with condition as the law directs, certificate is granted him for obtaining a probate thereof in due form.

Page 97.
Gerrard Hutt's Will

In the name of God, Amen, I Gerrard Hutt of Cople Parish and County of Westmoreland being weak in body but sound mind and memory do make constitute and appoint and ordain this to be my last will and testament in manner and form following.
Item I give and bequeath unto my loving wife Mary Hutt all my estate, viz; land, Negroes, stock of all claims, and household furniture during her life and after her death to be directed as followeth;
Item I give and bequeath to my grandson William Hutt my large case, my young bay mare, saddle and bridle, housing and clothes.
Item I give and bequeath to my grandson Gerrard Hutt, son of John Hutt, Negro girl Rose.
Item I give and bequeath to my grandson Joseph Read, son of Andrew Read and his heirs, two Negro girls, Let and Bet, together with one bed and furniture. In case my grandson dies underage without heirs then to go to the next surviving son of my daughter Mary Ann Read and for want of such heirs to be equally divided amongst the several children that shall be borne of the body of my daughter Mary Ann Read. It is my will and desire that the two Negroes shall remain in the hands of my executors until my grandson arrives to the age of 21 years.
Item I give and bequeath to my son Gerrard Hutt, four young cattle, Negro boy James and his father Davey.
Item I give and bequeath to my grandson Gerrard Hutt, son of Gerrard Hutt, four head of young cattle.
Item I give and bequeath to my grandson John Brown, son of William Brown, five Negroes: Jenny, Charles, Hanner, Nancy and Silvia and his heirs and for want of such heirs to return and be equally divided amongst all my children and grandchildren and the said Negro shall remain in the hands of my executors until my grandson arrives to the age of 21 years.
Item I give and bequeath to my son Gerrard Hutt all that tract of land that he now lives on together with 300 pounds current money to be paid out of my estate that is not already bequeath.
Item I give and bequeath to my grandson Joseph Read and his heirs all that tract of land I purchased of John Crabb formerly the property of Coleman Read and for want of such heirs to fall to the next heir male born of my daughter Mary Ann Read, and for want of such heirs to fall to my son Gerrard Hutt and his heirs.
Item I give and bequeath to my grandson John Brown and his heirs all that tract of land I purchased of John Robinson and for want of such heirs to fall to my son Gerard Hutt.
Item it is my will and desire that the remainder of my estate that is not already bequeath shall be equally divided between all my children and grandchildren after the death of my loving wife Mary Hutt.
Item I leave my sons John Hutt and Gerard Hutt executors of this my last will and testament.
In witness whereof I have hereunto set my hand and seal this 4th day of May 1770
Test. Gerard Hutt
Thomas Edwards
Traverse McGuire (his mark)
Thomas Blundell (his mark)
At a court held for Westmoreland County the 25th day of September 1770 this will was proved according to law by the oaths of Thomas Edwards, Traverse McGuire and Thomas Blundell the witnesses thereto and ordered to be recorded and on the motion of John Hutt and Gerrard Hutt the executors therein named who made oath thereto according to law together with Alexander Spark and Thomas Edwards their securities entered into and acknowledged bond with condition as the law directs, certificate is granted them for obtaining a probate thereof in due form. Teste James Davenport Clk Cur

Page 99.
Lamkin & Wife to Smith Indenture
This indenture made the 4th day of April 1770 between Matthew Lamkin and Frances Lamkin

his wife and Peter Lamkin of the County of Westmoreland and Parish of Cople of the one part and John Smith of the Parish of St. Stephen and County of Northumberland, Gent., of the other part. Witnessed that Matthew Lamkin and Frances Lamkin in consideration of 125 pounds current money of Virginia has sold to John Smith 3 acres of land and mill situated in the Parish of Cople and County of Westmoreland adjoining the mill now in possession of the said John Smith and commonly called and known by the name of Lamkin's Mill. In witness whereof the parties to these presents have set their hands and affixed their seals the day and year first above written.

Signed sealed and delivered in presence of
John Hobson Fallin, John Middleton
William Fleming, James Knott
Hugh Hamilton, Abraham Beacham
Patrick Ballantine

Matthew Lamkin
Frances Lamkin
Peter Lamkin

To Newton Keene, Rodham Kenner and Lindsay Opie. Whereas Matthew Lamkin, Frances his wife and Peter Lamkin by their indenture of bargain and sale bearing date the 4th day of April 1770 have sold and conveyed unto John Smith, Jr., Gent., The fee simple estate of a water grist mill with her appurtenances together with 3 acres of land thereto adjoining lying in the Parish of Cople and County of Westmoreland and whereas the said Frances Lamkin cannot conveniently travel to our County Court of Westmoreland to make acknowledgment of the conveyance. Therefore, we do give unto you or any two of you power to receive the acknowledgment which the said Frances Lamkin may be willing to make. Witness James Davenport, clerk of our said court at the courthouse aforesaid the 25th day of May.

Northumberland Sct. By virtue of the annexed commission, we the subscribers examined Mrs. Frances Lamkin, wife of Mr. Matthew Lamkin in regard to the mill and lands therein mentioned who freely consented to the said deed being recorded the office of the County of Westmoreland and now she the said Frances acknowledged that she did the same of her own free will and desire. Certified under our hands and seals this 26th day of May 1774.

Newton Keene
Lindsay Opie

At a court held for Westmoreland County 25th day of September 1770 this indenture and the receipt endorsed were proved by the oath of Abraham Beacham and he witness thereto and the same having been proved in June last by the oath of two other witnesses thereto are together with the commission annexed for taking the acknowledgment and privy examination of Frances Lamkin the wife of Matthew Lamkin party thereto and a certificate of the execution thereof, ordered to be recorded. Test

Page 102.

Triplett & Wife to Monroe Indenture

This indenture made the 19th day of August 1770 [1769] between John Triplett of the parish of Hanover and County of King George of the one part and George Monroe of Washington Parish and County of Westmoreland of the other part. Witnesseth that John Triplett and Martha Triplett his wife in consideration of 35 pounds current money of Virginia has sold to George Monroe a tract of land situate in the Parish of Washington and County of Westmoreland containing 96 acres and bounded as followeth; beginning at a white oak standing on the side of Jett's Mill, thence 86° East along a line of marked trees that divides the land from Prices, 172 poles thence North 118 pole to Piper's Rolling Road, thence up the said Road to Jett's Mill, thence to the beginning. In witness whereof the said John Triplett and Martha Triplett his wife hereunto set their hands and seals this [blank]

Signed sealed and delivered in presence of
William Monroe
Benjamin Steward
James Butler
William Butler

John Triplett
Martha Triplett (her mark)

William Kitton
To William Robinson and Horatio Dade, Gent. Whereas John Triplett and Martha Triplett his wife by their indenture of bargain and sale bearing date the 19th day of August 1769 have sold and conveyed unto George Monroe the fee simple estate of 96 acres with the appurtenances lying in the Parish of Washington and County of Westmoreland and whereas the said Martha Triplett cannot conveniently travel to our court of Westmoreland County to make acknowledgment of the conveyance. Therefore, we do give unto you or any two or more of you power to receive the acknowledgment which the said Martha Triplett shall be willing to make. Witness James Davenport, clerk of our said court the 1st day of October 1769.
King George County. Pursuant to the within writ to us directed dated the 1st day of this instant October have examined Martha Triplett, wife of John Triplett separate and apart from her husband and find her willing to relinquish her right of dower to a parcel of land in Westmoreland County sold by her husband John Triplett to George Monroe, Jr. Witness our hands this 25th day of October 1769.
William Robinson
Horatio Dade
At a court held for Westmoreland County the 27th day of November 1770 this indenture Feoffment in the memorandum of livery of seizen and receipt underwritten were proved by the oaths of William Monroe, James Butler and William Butler witnesses thereto and to gather with the commission annexed for taking the acknowledgment and privy examination of Martha Triplett the wife of John Triplett party thereto and a certificate of the execution thereof, ordered to be recorded. Teste

Page 106.
Spillman with Spillman Division of Land
A division made and indented this 27th day of October 1770. Whereas William Spillman, deceased, did by his last will give to his 3 sons, Thomas Spillman, William Spillman, and John Spillman, a dividend of land in the Parish of Washington and County of Westmoreland one tract of land between his three sons containing 200 or more acres, and as the aforesaid Thomas Spillman and William Spillman both purchased the one divided third part belonging to the said John Spillman, and both by consent made a division agreeable to themselves. Viz; beginning at the mouth of the Meadow Branch formerly called Whitins Meadow and running up the said branch to the main fork, thence North to the back line of the aforesaid tract of land that lot or parcel of land on the east side of the said branch and North line to belonged to Thomas Spillman and his heirs forever; and the other part or lot of land lying on the west side of the said branch and North line in the east side of the main branch of the head of Mattox to belonged to William Spillman;
Signed sealed and delivered in presence of us — Thomas Spillman
Peter Jett — William Spillman
At a court held for Westmoreland County the 27th day of November 1770 this indenture was acknowledged by Thomas Spillman and William Spillman parties thereto and ordered to be recorded. Test

Page 107.
Thomas Sanford's Will
In the name of God, Amen, I Thomas Sanford of Westmoreland County and the Parish of Cople being weak and sickly of body but of perfect mind and sound memory do make and ordain this my last will and testament in manner and form following.
Item I give to my grandson, Thomas Sanford, son of Youell Sanford and Elizabeth Sanford his wife, 150 acres of land, which said land my father formerly lived on and called by the name of Sanford's Old Fields and bounded on the land of Joseph Stone, Richard Moxley, Edward Sanford, and Youell Sanford. Which said land I give to him and his heirs and for

want of such heirs to descend to the next heir at law and to be possessed of the said lands after his father's death and not before and after all my debts being justly paid.
I give and bequeath to my loving wife Margaret Sanford all the rest of my whole estate consisting of stock, goods, movables and immovables for and during her natural life and after her death to be equally divided amongst any children then living and my grandson Thomas Luttrell whom I joined with my other children to receive his mother's part of my estate, and if it's so happen that my wife died before he comes to the age of 21 years, then each such part as shall be due to him to be lodged in my executors hands till he comes to the age of 21 years or day of marriage.
For the true performance of this my last will and testament I appoint my loving wife Margaret Sanford and my son Thomas Sanford executrix and Executor of this my will to see it justly completed in confirmation whereof I have hereunto set my hand and affixed my seal this 24th day of May 1767.
Signed sealed and delivered in presence of Thomas Sanford
Charles Sanford, Hannah Sturman
Edward Sanford
At a court held for Westmoreland County the 27th day of November 1770 this will was proved according to law by the oaths of Charles Sanford and Edward Sanford witnesses thereto and ordered to be recorded and on the motion of Thomas Sanford one of the executors therein named who made oath thereto according to law did together with the said Edward Sanford and Charles Sanford his securities entered into and acknowledged bond with condition as the law directs, certificate is granted him for obtaining a probate thereof in due form; liberty being reserved to the executrix therein named to join in the probate thereof when she shall think fit. Teste

Page 109.
John Muse's Will
In the name of God, Amen, the 11th day of October 1770, by John Muse of the County of Westmoreland being sick and weak in body but of perfect mind and memory do make and ordain this my last will and testament.
My body to be buried at the discretion of my executors, Richard Muse and Daniel Muse.
My desire is that my whole estate should be sold and any debts all discharged out of the money arising from the sale, and the surplus to be equally divided between my two sons Daniel Muse and James Muse except my riding mare, side saddle and feather bed which I give to my beloved wife Eleanor Muse during her life, in case there should be effects sufficient to discharge my debts without, and after her decease to descend to my two sons above mentioned. In witness whereof I have hereunto set my hand and seal the day and year above mentioned.
Signed and delivered in the presence of the subscribers John Muse (his mark)
Edward Muse
Elizabeth Muse (her mark)
At a court held for Westmoreland County the 27th day of November 1770 this will was proved according to law by the oath of Edward Muse and Elizabeth Muse the witnesses thereto and ordered to be recorded and on the motion of Richard Muse one of the executors therein named who made oath thereto according to law and together with William Smith his security entered into and acknowledged bond with condition as the law directs, certificate is granted him for obtaining a probate thereof in due form. Teste

Page 110.
Andrew Monroe's Will
In the name of God, Amen, I Andrew Monroe of Westmoreland County being in perfect health sense and memory.
Item I give my wife Margaret Monroe, 5 pounds to buy her a ring if she thinks proper and

also, I give her my chair and gray horse and to live in the house one year and to have her use of Negro Judy for a year. I do this that she may have time to get another house.
Item I give to my grandson Elliott Monroe the land I have in Loudoun [County] that I bought of John Elliott on the following conditions; that is in case he does not bring a suit against my grandson John Monroe for the land whereon my son John Monroe lived, now if Elliott Monroe or his heirs should bring any suit against my grandson John Monroe for the said lands in that case I give the above mentioned tract of land in Loudoun [County] to my grandson John Monroe his heirs forever; my meaning is that Elliott Monroe should have but one of the above mentioned parcels of land.
I also give Elliott Monroe the sixth part of all my Negroes after debts are paid but in case Elliott Monroe should die without issue then the above-mentioned land and Negroes to go to my grandson John Monroe.
I give to my grandson John Monroe all the land I live on and that is joining that piece back of Spence Monroe's which I took up, and also, the land in Frederick [County] that I have bought a suit against William Grayson for, to him and his heirs forever.
Item I give my grandson the above lands in lieu of the land I promised my son John Monroe in a marriage contract, that is in case, Elliott Monroe sues for the land mentioned in the contract and recovers it.
I also give my grandson John Monroe my gold watch to be always in the family.
I give all my clothes to my poor neighbors.
All the remainder part of my estate is to be equally divided between my four grandchildren after Elliott Monroe's part is taken out, Viz; John Monroe, Jane Monroe, Elizabeth Monroe and Nancy Monroe. Negro Patience is to be put in Nancy Monroe's part.
I give my executor full power to sell all the land I live on and all adjoining to it if they think it will be for my grandson John Monroe's interest and dispose of the money arising from the sale as they think fit most for my grandson John Monroe's interest.
I constitute and appoint my friends Dr. James Bankhead, John Ashton and Spence Monroe my executors to this my last will. As witness my hand and seal the 1st day of May 1769.
Sealed and delivered in presence of Andrew Monroe
William Berryman
William Berryman, Jr.
John Washington
NB I give the use of my mulatto girl Mary to my wife till she arrives to the age of 21 and then to my four youngest grandchildren.
At a court held for Westmoreland County the 27th day of November 1770 this will and the codicil underwritten were approved according to law by the oaths of William Berryman, Jr., and John Washington witnesses thereto and ordered to be recorded and on the motion of Spence Monroe one of the executors therein named who made oath thereto according to law and together with William Bernard and William Craighill his securities entered into and acknowledged bond with condition as the law directs, certificate is granted him for obtaining a probate thereof in due form. Teste

Page 111.
Washington & Wife to Turberville Lease
This indenture made the 8th day of January 1771 between Samuel Washington of the County of Frederick and colony of Virginia of the one part and John Turberville of the County of Westmoreland and colony of Virginia of the other part. Witnesseth that Samuel Washington in consideration of five shillings current money of Virginia has sold unto John Turberville a tract or dividend of land lying in the County of Westmoreland on the eastwardly side of Machodoc River and bounded by the lands of Robert Carter, Esq., Richard Lee, Esq., Leroy Griffin, Thomas Beale and John Crabb, the same being part of a greater tract of land estimated to contain 1878 acres formally the property of Willoughby Allerton, Gent and being all that part or dividend of land which was allotted to the said Samuel Washington in right of

his wife by a decree of the County Court of Westmoreland and the courses including the said part of land containing 878 acres. To have and to hold the lands unto the said John Turberville from the day before the date heretofore and during the full term of one year from thence next ensuing yielding and paying the rent of one pepper corn to the intent and purpose that by virtue of these presents and of the statute for transferring uses into possession the said John Turberville may be in actual possession of the premises and be there by enabled to accept and take a grant and release of the reversions and inheritance thereof. In witness whereof the said Samuel Washington has hereunto set his hand and seal the day and year first above written.

Sealed and delivered in the presence of Samuel Washington
Lawrence Washington, Jr.
John Augustine Washington
John Gordon
John Bryan

Page 112.
Washington & Wife Release to Turberville

This indenture made the 9th day of January 1771 between Samuel Washington and Anne Washington his wife of the County of Frederick and colony of Virginia of the one part and John Turberville of the County of Westmoreland and colony of Virginia of the other part. Witnesseth that Samuel Washington in consideration of 2000 pounds current money of Virginia has sold unto John Turberville in his actual possession now being by virtue of a bargain and sale to him made by the said Washington for one whole year by indenture bearing date the day next before the day of the date of these presents and by force of the statute for transferring uses into possession, a tract or dividend of land lying in the County of Westmoreland on the eastwardly side of Machodoc River and bounded by the lands of Robert Carter, Esq., Richard Lee, Esq., Leroy Griffin, Thomas Beale and John Crabb, the same being part of a greater tract of land estimated to contain 1878 acres formally the property of Willoughby Allerton, Gent and being all that part or dividend of land which was allotted to the said Samuel Washington in right of his wife by a decree of the County Court of Westmoreland and the courses including the said part of land containing 878 acres.

In witness whereof the said Samuel Washington and Anne Washington his wife have hereunto set their hands and seals the day and year first above written.

Sealed and delivered in the presence of Samuel Washington
Lawrence Washington, Jr. Anne Washington
John Augustine Washington
John Bryan
John Gordon

To Jacob Hite and Adam Stephens, Gent. Whereas Samuel Washington County of Frederick, Gent., and Anne Washington his wife by their indentures of lease and release bearing date the eighth and ninth days of January have sold and conveyed to John Turberville of the County of Westmoreland, Gent., The fee simple estate of a tract of land lying in the Parish of Cople and the County of Westmoreland containing [878] acres known by the name of Narrows and whereas the said Anne Washington cannot conveniently travel to record of our said County of Westmorland to make acknowledgment of the said conveyance. Therefore, we do give unto you or any two of you power to receive the acknowledgment which the said Anne Washington shall be willing to make. Witness James Davenport, clerk of our said court the 11th day of January.

Frederick County Sct. We hereby certify that in consequence of the within commission we have waited upon Anne Washington and have examined her apart and in private from Samuel Washington her husband and she does freely and willingly without persuasions or threats three to the sale of the lands and is willing they shall be admitted to record in the court of Westmoreland. Given under our hands and seals this 10th day of January 1771.

Jacob Hite
Adam Stephens
At court held for Westmoreland County the 26th day of March 1771 this indenture of lease and release and a receipt written under the said release were presented by the oaths of Lawrence Washington, Sr., John Augustine Washington and John Bryan witnesses thereto and together with the commission the next for taking the acknowledgment and privy examination of Anne Washington the wife of Samuel Washington, Gent., thereto and a certificate of the execution thereof ordered to be recorded. Teste

Page 116.
Matthew Partridge's Will
In the name of God, Amen, I Matthew Partridge of Cople Parish and County of Westmoreland being weak in body but of sound memory do this 13th day of November 1770 make and publish this my last will and testament in manner following.
Imprimis, I give to my two sons Richard Partridge and Matthew Partridge and their heirs the following Negroes; Winny, Sarah, Sam, Little Sarah and Symon; and their increase to be equally divided when they arrive to the age of 21 years.
Item I give and bequeath to each of my three daughters, Sally Partridge, Jenny Partridge and Patty Partridge one full fifth part of my whole estate to be paid them by my two sons as they shall marry or arrive to the full age of 18 years.
Item I give and bequeath unto my loving wife Jemima Partridge, my bay mare she commonly rides, and it is my will and desire that my estate should be kept together until my sons arrive to the age of 21 years, and the crops made by my said Negroes, after paying the rents and all my just debts, finding tools, clothing my wife and children and Negroes, then the money that is made by said crops, to be for to pay my daughters part as far as it will as they marry or arrive to the age of 18 years.
Lastly, I do make and ordain my friend Mr. Daniel Morgan executor of this my last will and testament. In witness whereof I have hereunto set my hand and seal the day and year above written.
Signed sealed and delivered in presence of us Matthew Partridge
Reuben Jordan
John Minor
Sarah Webb (her mark)
Betty Coward (her mark)
At a court held for Westmoreland County the 24th day of March 1771, this will was proved according to law by the oath of John Minor and witness thereto and ordered to be recorded and on the motion of Daniel Morgan the executor therein named who made oath thereto according to law and together with John Rust and William Barecroft, his securities entered into and acknowledged bond with condition as the law directs, certificate is granted him for obtaining a probate thereof in due form. Previous to which, Jemima Partridge, the widow and relict of the testator personally appeared in court and absolutely renounced all benefit or advantage which she might claim under the said will. Teste

Page 117.
John Higdon's Will
I John Higdon of the County of Westmoreland do make and ordain this my last will and testament in manner and form following.
Imprimis, I give to my son John Higdon my gun.
Item I give all the rest of my estate (after my debts are paid) be equally divided among my four children; Elizabeth Higdon, Original Higdon, John Higdon and Richard Higdon to be equally divided between them.
Lastly, I hereby appoint Mr. Thomas Jett executor to this my last will and testament. In witness whereof I have hereunto set my hand and seal this 23rd day of December 1770.

Signed sealed published in the presence of John Higdon
William Fisher
John Fisher
At a court held for Westmoreland County the 28th day of March 1771 this will was proved according to law by the oaths of William Fisher and John Fisher the witnesses thereto and ordered to be recorded and on the motion of Thomas Jett the executor therein named who made oath thereto according to law and together with Daniel McCarty is security entered into and acknowledged bond with condition as the law directs, certificate is granted him for obtaining a probate thereof in due form. Teste

Page 118.
Charles Lawrence Will
In the name of God, Amen, I Charles Lawrence of the County of Westmoreland being of a sound and disposing mind and memory do make and ordain this my last will and testament in manner and form following.
Item I give and bequeath unto my cousin William Lawrence all my whole estate in whatever it consists and by means my cousin that lives with me which is Junior.
Lastly, I do make my said cousin William Lawrence, Jr., my sole executor of this my last will and testament dated this first day of May 1770.
Signed and sealed and delivered in presence of us Charles Lawrence (his mark)
Benjamin Settle
Telif Alverson
Mary Atwell (her mark)
At a court held for Westmoreland County the 26th day of March 1770 one this will was proved according to law by the oaths of Telif Alverson and Mary Atwell witnesses thereto and ordered to be recorded and on the motion of William Lawrence the executor therein named who made oath thereto according to law and together with Benjamin Settle and Matthew Welch his securities entered into and acknowledged bond with condition as the law directs, certificate is granted him for obtaining a probate thereof in due form. Teste

Page 119.
Moxley to Moxley Agreement
I John Moxley of the County of Westmoreland for the love and affection which I have and do bear to my son Augustine Moxley of the County aforesaid do freely and truly give by these presents my Negro man Azzurn for and during my natural life, he paying me the sum of 1000 pounds of neat tobacco yearly and every year during the said term, clear of all charges. I do also make over to my said son my whole estate of all and every kind which I have at present or may be possessed of at the time of my death, he paying all my debts which I owe, on these conditions my whole estate is to be his and his heirs and assigns forever. In confirmation whereof I have hereunto set my hand and seal this 26th day of February 1771.
Signed sealed and delivered in the presence of us John Moxley (his mark)
Augustine Sanford
Willoughby Sanford
At a court held for Westmoreland County the 26th day of March 1771 this deed was proved by the oaths of Augustine Sanford and Willoughby Sanford the witnesses thereto and ordered to be recorded. Teste

Page 119.
Benedict Middleton's Will
Westmoreland County, Cople Parish
I Benedict Middleton, son of Robert Middleton, make and ordain constitute and appoint this my last will and testament in manner and form as followeth.
Item I give and bequeath to my loving brother John Middleton all my land, he paying any just

debts and 40 pounds to my brother William Middleton and for want of such issue to my brother William Middleton and the issue of his body.
My will is that all the residue of my estate be sold and equally divided between my brother Robert Middleton and my two cousins Mary Rust and Elizabeth Rust.
I ordain constitute and appoint my loving brother John Middleton whole and sole executor of this my last will and testament.
In witness whereof I have hereunto set my hand and seal this 22nd day of September 1770.
Test
William Pynsent Wordsman? Benedict Middleton
William Fleming
Benedict Middleton
At a court held for Westmoreland County the 26th day of March 1771 this will was proved according to law by the oaths of William Fleming and Benedict Middleton witnesses thereto and ordered to be recorded and on the motion of John Middleton the executor therein named who made oath thereto according to law and together with George Rust his security entered into and acknowledged bond with condition as the law directs, certificate is granted him for obtaining a probate thereof in due form. Teste
[Sir William Pynsent, Somerset, England died w/o heir]

Page 120.
Elizabeth Brown's Will
In the name of God Amen, I Elizabeth Brown the County of Westmoreland and Parish of Washington being sick and weak but of disposing mind and memory do make constitute and appoint this my last will and testament in manner and form following.
Item I give and devise to my loving brother James Dishman my land where I now live.
Item I give and devise to my loving sister Mary Rutherford the bed and furniture that I commonly sleep on myself.
Item I give and devise to my said brother James Dishman all the rest of my estate after my just debts are paid consisting of personal and real. Also, I appoint my brother James Dishman executor of this my will this 30th day of August 1770
Signed and sealed in the presence of Elizabeth Brown (her mark)
William Piper
Peter Jett
William Kiln?
At a court held for Westmoreland County the 28th day of May 1771 this will was proved according to law by the oaths William Piper and Peter Jett witnesses thereto and ordered to be recorded and on the motion of James Dishman the executor therein named who made oath thereto according to law and together with William Piper his security entered into and acknowledged bond with condition as the law directs, certificate is granted him for obtaining a probate thereof in due form. Teste

Page 121.
John Cussingheiffer's Will [Cupingheifer]
In the name of God, Amen, this 13th day of February 1771, I John Cussingheiffer of County of Westmoreland and Parish of Washington being very sick and weak but of perfect sense and memory do hereby make and ordain this my last will and testament in manner and form following.
Item I do leave all my living to my wife Mary Cussingheiffer as long as she lives, after her death then to be equally divided amongst my several children; Mical Cussingheiffer, Hannah Cussingheiffer, and John Cussingheiffer.
My desire is that my son John Cussingheiffer is to have five years schooling and to be paid out of my living and if my wife should not live to see my children of lawful age then my desire is that my brother Jacob Cussingheiffer should have the care and management of my

children.
In witness whereof I have hereunto set my hand and seal the day and date above written.
Teste Frances Jarvis John Cussingheiffer
John Jarvis
At a court held for Westmoreland County the 28th day of May 17701 this last will and testament of John Cussingheiffer, deceased was proved according to law by the oaths of Frances Jarvis and John Jarvis the witnesses thereto and ordered to be recorded and no executor being named in the said will, on the motion of Mary Cussingheiffer, the widow of the said John Cussingheiffer, who made oath thereto according to law and together with John Chancellor and George Shoats her securities entered into and acknowledged bond with condition as the law directs, certificate is granted her for obtaining letters of administration with the said will the next in due form. Teste

Page 122.
Matthew Bayne's Will
In the name of God, Amen, the second day of March 1769 I Matthew Bayne of the County of Westmoreland although weak in body yet of sound and perfect mind and memory do constitute make and ordain this my last will and testament in manner and form as follows.
Imprimis, I leave to my loving wife the use of all my whole estate both real and personal within doors and without, during her remaining a widow or otherwise till her death and after her intermarriage or deceased to be disposed of in the following manner and form.
Item I give and bequeath to my son Matthew Bayne my tract of land that I now live on which I purchased of William Bridges, deceased, and my Negro wench Nann and my Negro boy Jessey.
Item I give and bequeath to my son Caron Bayne all my lands that I purchased of the Pope's and also a tract of land that I purchased of Nathaniel Butler; except that my daughter Sarah Vigour shall live upon the said tract of land that I purchased of Nathaniel Butler during her widowhood; and also, my Negro man Great Dick and my Negro wench Jenny.
Item I give and bequeath to my son William Bayne my tract of land I purchased of John Higdon, my Negro man Little Dick and my Negro boy Jesse.
Item I give and bequeath to my son Richard Bayne, Negro boy Charles during his natural life and after his decease to return to his daughter Mary Bayne.
Item I give and bequeath to my son John Bayne, 30 pounds to be paid him by my executors within nine months after my will is recorded and that my son have no more of my estate besides what I have already given him.
Item I give and bequeath to my son Daniel Bayne, Negro boy Jack during his natural life and after his decease to return to his daughter Anne Bayne.
Item I give and bequeath to my son George Bayne, Negro boy Clark.
Item I give and bequeath to my Daughter Sarah Vigour, Negro wench Lucy and her increase during her natural life and after her decease to return to the heirs of William Vigour.
Item I give and bequeath to my daughter Amy Bridges, Negro boy Natt during her natural life and after her life to return to her son Matthew Bridges.
Item I give and devise to my daughter Elizabeth Bayne, Negro boys Toney and Tom.
Item I give and bequeath to my two sons, Matthew Bayne and Cason Bayne in copartnership my still, kettle and worm.
Item my will and desire is that the profits that shall arise from the labor of my slaves after my decease during the time that my wife shall be possessed, shall be solely at her disposal to give to whomsoever she shall think fit.
Item I give and bequeath all the remainder part of my estate not before mentioned to be equally divided between my four children, Matthew Bayne, Caron Bayne, William Bayne and Elizabeth Bayne. And my will and desire is that my daughter Elizabeth Bayne should live and remain in my mansion house as usual till her intermarriage.
Item my will and desire is that if any of the legacies before mentioned in my will should die

without an heir then the legacies devised to them should return and be equally divided between my four children, Matthew Bayne, Caron Bayne, William Bayne and Elizabeth Bayne.

I appoint, ordain and constitute my beloved wife Eleanor Bayne, my son Matthew Bayne and my son Caron Bayne to be my executors of this my last will and testament. In witness whereof I have hereunto set my hand and affixed my seal the day month and year first above written.

Signed sealed published in presence of Matthew Bayne
George Payne
William Berkley
Charles Poor (his mark)

At a court held for Westmoreland County the 28th day of May 1771 this will was proved according to law by the oaths of George Payne and Charles Poor witnesses thereto and ordered to be recorded and on the motion of Eleanor Bayne, widow and executrix named in the said will who made oath thereto according to law and together with Caron Bayne and Matthew Bayne her securities entered into and acknowledged bond with condition as the law directs, certificate is granted her for obtaining a probate thereof in due form, Matthew Bayne and Caron Bayne the other executors named in the said will personally appeared and refused to take upon themselves the burthen of the execution thereof. Teste

Page 124.

George Monroe's Will

In the name of God, Amen, I George Monroe, Jr., being sick and weak of body but of perfect memory do now make this my last will and testament as follows.

In the first place I give and bequeath to my loving wife Peggy Monroe, my Negro woman Sarah.

Item I give and bequeath to my loving son William Monroe the land I first purchased of Col. John Triplett containing 200 acres to him and his heirs and for want of heirs to his brother George Monroe.

Item I give and bequeath to my loving son George Monroe the plantation I now live on being the land I purchased of Capt. John Triplett containing 95 acres to him and his heirs and for want of heirs to his brother John Monroe.

Item I give and bequeath to my loving son John Monroe the second purchase of land I made of Col. John Triplett whereon Thomas Bridges now lives containing 200 acres to him and his heirs and for want of such heirs to his brother William Monroe.

Item I give and bequeath to my loving daughter Mary Monroe the land I made an entry of in the year 1769 binding on John Price's land and the land of Samuel White to her and her heirs and for want of such heirs to my daughter Sarah Monroe and her heirs and for want of heirs to my daughter Ann Monroe and her heirs.

Item my desire is that my whole estate to be kept together until my son William Monroe comes to the age of 21 years and remain in the possession of my loving wife in case she lives a widow for the better to enable her to raise and school my children, provided there is no visible appearance of waste and at the time of my son William Monroe coming to the age of 21 years my will and desire is that all my slaves and their increase and all my personal estate be equally divided betwixt my six children; William Monroe, George Monroe, John Monroe, Mary Monroe, Sarah Monroe, and Ann Monroe. Except the wench Sarah, already devised to my wife and her increase in my wife's dower.

I nominate and appoint my loving wife, my loving brother William Monroe and my friend Spence Monroe, executrix and executors of this my last will and testament. In witness whereof I have hereunto set my hand and seal this 12th day of November 1770.

In the presence of George Monroe (his mark)
John Weedon, John Weedon, Jr.
William Dishman, Andrew Monroe

John Monroe, William Butler
At a court held for Westmoreland County the 25th day of June 1771 this will was proved according to law by the oaths of John Weedon, Jr., John Monroe and William Butler witnesses thereto and ordered to be recorded and on motion of Peggy Monroe, widow and executrix therein named who made oath thereto according to law and together with William Butler and Charles Morris her securities entered into and acknowledged bond with condition as the law directs, certificate is granted her for obtaining a probate thereof in due form; liberty been reserve to the executors therein named to join in the probate thereof when they shall think fit. Teste

Page 126.
Johnson from Vowles Indenture
This indenture made the third day of April 1771 between Richard Vowles of the Parish of Washington and County of Westmoreland of the one part and George Johnson of the county and parish aforesaid of the other part. Witnesseth that Richard Vowles in consideration of sum of 110 pounds current money has sold unto George Johnson a parcel of land lying in the upper end of the county aforesaid containing a tract of land purchased by the said Richard Vowles of Robert Peck and Thomas Stribling and their respective wife's containing 107 acres the bounds of which are also mentioned in the said deed. In witness whereof the said Richard Vowles hath hereunto set his hand and seal the day and year above mentioned.
Signed sealed and acknowledge in presence of Richard Vowles
John Bryan, Sr., William Settle
Joseph Bryan, Alexander Grant (his mark)
Richard Rollings (his mark), Joseph Rollings (his mark)
William Bernard, Alexander Rose
Edward Ransdell, Jr.
Joseph Peirce, William Nelson
At a court held for Westmoreland County the 25th day of June 1771 this indenture and the receipt underwritten were proved by the oaths of Alexander Rose, Edward Ransdell, Jr., Joseph Peirce and William Nelson witnesses thereto and ordered to be recorded. Test

Page 128.
Walker to Middleton Indenture
This indenture made this 19th day of September 1770 between Alice Walker of the Parish of Lunenburg and County of Richmond of the one part and Robert Middleton of the Parish of Cople and the County of Westmoreland of the other part witnesseth that Thomas Walker, grandfather to the aforesaid Alice Walker, late of the Parish of Cople and the County of Westmoreland, deceased, by virtue of a deed passed to him by Robert Middleton of the parish and County aforesaid, deceased bearing date the 25th day of August 1686 stood seized at his death of 150 acres of land lying in the parish and county aforesaid and bounded as followeth; beginning at a red oak by a path being the corner and beginning tree of the said Robert Middleton, extending thence South 22° East 20 poles to a corner red oak on a branch from thence, North 40° East 170 poles, to a hickory corner tree of Richard Dunahaugh [Dunahew], from thence South 75° East 48 poles to a red oak corner tree to the said Richard Dunahaugh [Dunahew] and George Lamkin, from thence South 32° East 27 poles to a red oak, thence South 45° West bounding southeasterly the land of Frances Clay 232 poles to a red oak corner tree of the said Clay and Robert Middleton, thence West 132 poles to a red oak standing in the said Middleton's line of and from thence along the said Middleton's line North 45° East 140 poles to the beginning tree. Which said 150 acres of land the said Thomas Walker gave and bequeath to his son Benjamin Walker father to the said Alice Walker by his last will and testament bearing the date the 26th day of January 1710., and the said Benjamin Walker departed this life without making any will, whereby the aforesaid 150 acres of land descended to his daughters; Seleashea Walker, Mary Jeffries Walker and Alice

Walker, they being coheirs. Now this indenture witness that Alice Walker in consideration of 40 pounds current money of Virginia has sold to Robert Middleton all her estate, right, title and interest in to the said 150 acres of land. In witness whereof she hath hereunto set her hand and seal the day and year above written.
Signed sealed and delivered in presence of Alice Walker (her mark)
George Rust
Zachariah White
Seleashea White
At a court held for Westmoreland County the 25th day of June 1771 this indenture and the receipt thereon endorsed were proved by the oaths of Zachariah White and Seleashea White witnesses thereto and the same having been before proved by the old the other witnesses are ordered to be recorded. Teste

Page 131.
Adam Weaver's Will
In the name of God, Amen, I Adam Weaver of Cople Parish and County of Westmoreland, planter being weak of body but sound sense and perfect memory do make and ordain and declare this to be last will and testament in manner and form following.
Item I give to my loving wife Annaminor [Jemima?] all my estate during her life then to be equally divided among my children as followeth; John Weaver, William Weaver, Abraham Weaver, Benjamin Weaver, Zacharias Weaver, Elizabeth Bott, Mary Mothershead, and Hannah Weaver. But if my Negro fellow Brister that I have made a deed of gift to my son Benjamin Weaver should live till after my decease and my wife, then my son Benjamin Weaver to have his choice of my two guns and no more but the said Negro above mentioned.
Item I give to my son in law William Walker on shilling sterling and no more.
Item I give to my son in law William Jyles one shilling sterling and no more.
Item I give to my son John Weaver a young mare and gun I lent him which he is now in possession of.
Lastly, I constitute and appoint my two sons, John Weaver and Benjamin Weaver, executors of this my last will and testament. In witness whereof I have hereunto set my hand and affixed my seal this 30th day of November 1770.
Signed sealed and published in presence of us Adam Weaver (his mark)
William Omohundro
John Omohundro
At a court held for Westmoreland County the 25th day of June 1771 this will was proved according to law by the oaths of William Omohundro and John Omohundro the witnesses thereto and ordered to be recorded, and on the motion of John Weaver, one of the executors therein named who made oath thereto according to law and together with John Omohundro his security, entered into and acknowledged bond with condition as the law directs, certificate is granted him for obtaining a probate thereof in due form.

Page 132.
Turberville to Gill Lease
This indenture made the 17th of June 1771 between John Turberville of the County of Westmoreland, Gent., of the one part and Edward Gill of the Parish of Cople and County of Westmoreland, planter of the other part. Witnesseth that John Turberville in consideration of the rents and conditions has demised and to farm let unto Edward Gill, one tenement of land containing by estimation 127 acres, lying in the Parish of Cople and County of Westmoreland known by the name of Beards Old Field. To have and to hold tenement and appurtenances unto for and during the term of natural lives of him the said Edward Gill and Sarah Gill his now wife and to the survivor or longest liver of them, yielding and paying yearly and every year on the 25th day of December, if demanded, the net quantity of 1000 pounds of good crop tobacco and cask, the said tobacco to be paid at such convenient warehouse in the said

County of Westmoreland as the law shall appoint for the payment of tobacco debts. In witness whereof the parties within named to these presents have hereunto interchangeably set their hands and seals the day and year first within written.

Signed sealed and delivered in presence of — John Turberville
Jeane Corbin — Edward Gill
Gawin Corbin
David Wardrobe

At a court held for Westmoreland County 25th day of June 1771 this indenture was acknowledged by John Turberville and Edward Gill parties thereto and ordered to be recorded. Teste

Page 135.
Garrard to Payne Indenture

This indenture made the 12th day of December 1770 between James Garrard of the Parish of Overwharton and County of Stafford and Elizabeth Garrard his wife of one part and George Payne of the Parish of Washington and County of Westmoreland of the other part. Witnesseth that James Garrard and Elizabeth Garrard his wife in consideration of 80 pounds Virginia currency has sold to George Payne all that piece of land lying in the Parish of Washington and County of Westmoreland, formerly the property of James Naughty, the elder, who devised the same by his will to his son John Naughty and for want of heirs it became the property of James Garrard, party to this present indenture, as heir at law to the said John Naughty. Beginning at a white oak standing in the line of the land formerly belonging to William Quisenbury, extending along the said Quisenbury's line South East by East 70 poles, thence South 64° East 20 poles, thence South South East 40 pole, thence South 3° East 20 poles, thence South South West 40 pole to the head of a branch, then crossing the main road South 39 ½° East 37 poles to a corner tree, known by the name of Daniel O'Canny's corner, standing by a swamp side extending thence over the swamp North 62° East 180 poles to a little marked red oak standing of the South side of the main road in the line of Matthew Bayne, thence along the said Bayne's line North 15° West 110 pole to a corner tree on the South Easternmost side of a hill as it is supposed standing in the line of Philip Ludlow Lee, thence West 234 poles to the first mentioned white oak begun at.

In witness whereof the said parties to these presents have interchangeably set their hands and seals the day and year first above written.

Signed sealed and delivered in presence of — James Garrard
Margaret Stone
John Bayne
William Bayne, John Washington

At a court held for Westmoreland County the 25th day of June 1771, this indenture and receipt endorsed were proved by the oaths of John Bayne, William Bayne and John Washington, witnesses thereto and ordered to be recorded. Teste

Page 137.
Muse & Wife to Muse Indenture

This indenture made the 25th day of June 1771 between Nicholas Muse of the County of Westmoreland, planter and Margaret Muse his wife of the one part and James Muse of the same county of the other part. Witnesseth that Richard Muse and Margaret Muse his wife in consideration of 107 pounds current money of Virginia have sold to James Muse all that tract lying in the Parish of Washington and County of Westmoreland containing 111 acres, 2 rods and 30 poles bounded as followeth; beginning at a marked chestnut sapling, standing on the North side of a branch called Massey's Branch and running North 21° 45 minutes West 111 pole along the line dividing this land from that of Col. Fitzhugh's, thence South 55 ½° West 144 ½ pole along a new line of marked trees made by the said Richard Muse and James Muse as a dividing line between hem, to a stake standing in the side of a hill, then South 44°

East 127 pole to Massey's Branch, then up the several courses and meanders of the said run or branch to the beginning. This being part of a tract of 200 acres was sold and conveyed to the said Richard Muse by Thomas Morton and Anne Morton his wife by indenture bearing date the 30th day of September 1766. In witness whereof the parties to these presents have hereunto set their hands and seals the day and year above written.

Sealed and delivered in presence of — Richard Muse
Thomas Franklin — Margaret Muse
Joseph Moxley

At a court held for Westmoreland County the 28th day of June 1771 this indenture was acknowledged by Richard Muse and Margaret Muse his wife parties thereto, she being first privy examined as the law directs, and ordered to be recorded. Teste.

Page 138.
Chilton to Holbrooke Indenture

This indenture made the 26th day of April 1771 between Thomas Chilton of the Parish of Cople and County of Westmoreland of the one part and Mordecai Holbrooke of the parish and county aforesaid of the other part. Witnesseth that Thomas Chilton in consideration of their yearly rents and covenants [to be performed] has demised and to farm let unto Mordecai Holbrooke during his natural life and the lives of Dorothy Holbrooke his wife, and his son Joseph Holbrooke, 157 acres of land in the aforesaid County of Westmoreland and bounded as follows; beginning at a marked white oak standing near the road, at the head of the White Marsh and running northwestwardly along the said road 154 poles to Chilton's Mill Road, thence along the said mill road., North 75° East 14 ¾ pole, then North 64° East 70 ½ pole, then North 41 ½° East 33 pole, thence North 60° East 32 pole, then North 19° East 24 pole to a locust post standing near the said Holbrooke's dwelling house, then North 53° West 12 8/10 poles to a marked white oak standing near the brow of a hill, and near the main run, then North 72° East 44 poles to a marked testament, thence South 82° East 46 8/10 poles to a marked red oak, thence South 69 ¾° East 70 pole to a marked white oak standing on the side of a run that divides this land from the land of Robert Sanford, thence up to the said run to a line dividing this land from the said Robert Sanford's land, thence along the said line South West 72 pole to a marked spanish oak, thence South 41° East 50 pole to a marked white oak, a chestnut and a poplar, being corner to the said Robert Sanford, thence South 20° West 48 pole to the first beginning red oak at the head of the White Marsh. To have and to hold the said plantation yielding and paying yearly and every year during their natural lives on the first day of January in each year 630 pounds of crop tobacco and the quit rents, and plant under a sufficient fence 50 apple trees and 50 peach trees and shall not work more than five tithable besides himself on the said premises and shall not keep an ordinary or tipping house without asking the said Thomas Chilton. In witness whereof the parties to these presents have hereunto set their hands and seals the day and year above written.

Signed sealed and delivered in presence of — Thomas Chilton
John Cunningham — Mordecai Holbrooke (his mark)
William Griggs

At a court continued and held for Westmoreland County the 24th day of June 1771 this indenture was acknowledged by Thomas Chilton and Mordecai Holbrooke parties thereto and ordered to be recorded.

Page 140.
Sanford to Sanford Deed of Gift

I Willoughby Sanford for the love and affection which I have and do bear to my four children; Ann Sanford, Elizabeth Sanford, Mary Butler Harrison Sanford and John Sanford, do give the following things and slaves, to wit;

I do give to my daughter Ann Sanford, her mother's side saddle with all the furniture thereto belonging and likewise her mother's two gold rings the same to be delivered to her when she

comes of age or at the day of marriage.
I do give to my daughter Elizabeth Sanford, Negro man Ben.
I do give to my daughter Mary Butler Harrison Sanford, Negro girl Sarah and her future increase.
I do give to my son John Sanford, Negro boy Charles at my decease.
In confirmation whereof I have hereunto set my hand and affixed my seal this 30th day July 1771.
Signed sealed and delivered in the presence of us Willoughby Sanford
William Hazlerigg
Augustine Sanford
At a court held for Westmoreland County 30th day of July 1771 this deed of gift was proved by the oaths of William Hazlerigg and Augustine Sanford the witnesses thereto and ordered to be recorded. Teste

Page 141.
Grinnon to Bayne Indenture
This indenture bargain and sale of land made the 30th day of November 1770 between William Grinnon and Nancy Grinnon his wife of St. Mary's County and the province of Maryland and John Bayne of the Parish of Washington and County of Westmoreland of the other part. Witnesseth that William Grinnon and Nancy Grinnon his wife in consideration of 15 pounds Virginia currency has sold to John Bayne a parcel of land containing 60 acres formerly in the possession of William Chambers and son of William Chambers the refuted brother of Robert Chambers lying in the County of Westmoreland and Parish of Washington and binding on one of the branches of Pope's Creek, bounded as followeth; beginning at a marked chestnut and line of Philip Smith near and upon the swamp commonly known by the Beaver Dam, extending from thence along the said Smith's line to a red oak corner tree to this land and the land John Bushrod purchased of William Chambers son of Thomas Chambers, from thence along a line of marked trees which divides this land and the land (for mentioned) sold by William Chambers to John Bushrod until it intersects with the said Beaver Dam, finally from thence up the several meanders of the said Beaver Dam Run to the place begun at. In witness whereof the day and date above mentioned.
Signed sealed and delivered in presence of William Grinnon
Samuel Swann, Catherine Swann
Henry Swann, William Gray
William Muse, Richard Neuter
Matthew Bayne, Justinian Cooksey (his mark)
William Smith, John Jarvis
At a court held for Westmoreland County 30th day July 1771 this indenture was proved by the oath of William Smith a witness thereto and the said indenture with the receipt endorsed having been proved by two of the witnesses in March last are ordered to be recorded.
Teste; James Davenport CWC

Page 143.
Scutt & Wife to Turberville Indenture
This indenture made this sixth day of April 1771 between Thomas Scutt and Sarah Scutt his wife of the Parish of Cople and County of Westmoreland of the one part and John Turberville of the aforesaid Parish and County of the other part. Witnessed that Thomas Scutt and Sarah Scutt his wife in consideration of 22 [20 on receipt] pounds current money of Virginia has sold to John Turberville all that tract of land containing by estimation 51 acres lying in the aforesaid Parish of Cople and County of Westmoreland and is bounded as followeth; beginning at a red oak corner tree to John Turberville, Philip Smith who married Elizabeth Bushrod and the land of Lewin Bennett Garlick who married Elizabeth Dunkin who was sister and coheir with Sarah Scutt party to these presents, thence South to a poplar tree near the

said Smith's land and Dunkin's, thence West along a line between Smith and Dunkin to a white oak corner tree between Smith and the other half of Duncan's land (now Garlick's) thence along the line of trees being the dividing line of the said tract, to a white oak by the side of the old road and on the line of the aforesaid John Turberville's land, thence east along the said line to the beginning. In witness whereof the said parties to these presents have interchangeably set their hands and seals the day and year first above written.
Sealed and delivered in the presence of Sarah Scutt (her mark)
Thomas Welch Thomas Scutt
Benjamin Settle
Benjamin Brooks
James Habron
At a court held for Westmoreland County the 28th day of August 1771 this indenture together with the memorandum of livery of season and the receipt endorsed were acknowledged by Thomas Scutt and Sarah Scutt his wife parties thereto (she being first privy examined as the law directs) and ordered to be recorded. Test

Page 146.
McCarty & Wife to Quisenbury Indenture
This indenture made the 24th day of September 1771 Daniel McCarty and Winifred McCarty his wife of the Parish of Washington and County of Westmoreland and James Quisenbury of the same parish and county of the other part. Witnesseth that Daniel McCarty and Winifred McCarty his wife in consideration of 60 pounds current money of Virginia has sold to James Quisenbury a tract of land lying and being upon the north side of Monroe's Creek in the County of Westmoreland (which land the said McCarthy purchased of Thomas Whiting's executors) containing 60 acres. In witness whereof the said Daniel McCarty and Winifred McCarty his wife have hereunto set their hands and seals this day and year above written.
Signed sealed and delivered in presence of Daniel McCarty
William Nelson Winifred McCarty
P. Thornton
Baynham Burch
Nicholas Quisenbury
To John Martin, William Bernard and Philip Smith, Gent. Whereas Daniel McCarty and Winifred McCarty his wife by their indenture of bargain and sale bearing even date with these presents have sold and conveyed unto James Quisenbury the fee simple estate of 60 acres of land with the appurtenances lying in the Parish of Washington and the County of Westmoreland and whereas the said Winifred McCarty cannot conveniently travel to our court of Westmoreland County to make acknowledgment. Therefore, we do give unto you or any two or more of you power to receive the acknowledgment which the said Winifred McCarty shall be willing to make. Witness James Davenport, clerk of our said court the 24th day of September 1771.
Westmoreland Sct. Pursuant to the above dedimus directed to us, we privately examined Mrs. Winifred McCarty wife of Mr. Daniel McCarty of the County aforesaid to know if she willingly and without compulsion relinquished her right in a certain tract of land in the county aforesaid sold by the said McCarty to James Quisenbury of the County aforesaid. Given under our hands this 24th day of September 1771.
John Martin
Philip Smith
At a court held for Westmoreland County 24th day of September 1771 this indenture and receipt endorsed proved by the oaths of William Nelson, P. Thornton, and Baynham Burch, witnesses thereto and together with the commission annexed for taking the acknowledgment and privy examination Winifred McCarty the wife of Daniel McCarty, Gent., party thereto and a certificate of the execution thereof ordered to be recorded. Teste

Page 149.
McCarty & Wife to Quisenbury Indenture
This indenture made the 24th day of September 1771 Daniel McCarty and Winifred McCarty his wife of the Parish of Washington and County of Westmoreland and Nicholas Quisenbury of the same parish and county of the other part. Witnesseth that Daniel McCarty and Winifred McCarty his wife in consideration of 68 pounds current money of Virginia has sold to Nicholas Quisenbury a tract of land lying and being upon the north side of Monroe's Creek in the County of Westmoreland which land the said McCarthy came to by inheritance, containing 68 acres. In witness whereof the said Daniel McCarty and Winifred McCarty his wife have hereunto set their hands and seals this day and year above written.
Signed sealed and delivered in presence of Daniel McCarty
William Nelson Winifred McCarty
P. Thornton
Baynham Burch
James Quisenbury
To John Martin, William Bernard and Philip Smith, Gent. Whereas Daniel McCarty and Winifred McCarty his wife by their indenture of bargain and sale bearing even date with these presents have sold and conveyed unto Nicholas Quisenbury the fee simple estate of 68 acres of land with the appurtenances lying in the Parish of Washington and the County of Westmoreland and whereas the said Winifred McCarty cannot conveniently travel to our court of Westmoreland County to make acknowledgment. Therefore, we do give unto you or any two or more of you power to receive the acknowledgment which the said Winifred McCarty shall be willing to make. Witness James Davenport, clerk of our said court the 24th day of September 1771.
Westmoreland Sct. Pursuant to the above dedimus directed to us, we privately examined Mrs. Winifred McCarty wife of Mr. Daniel McCarty, Gent., her husband and acknowledged the indenture hereunto annexed to Nicholas Quisenbury of the freely and voluntarily without his persuasion or threats. Given under our hands this 24th day of September 1771.
John Martin
Philip Smith
At a court held for Westmoreland County 24th day of September 1771 this indenture and receipt endorsed proved by the oaths of William Nelson, P. Thornton, and Baynham Burch, witnesses thereto and together with the commission annexed for taking the acknowledgment and privy examination Winifred McCarty the wife of Daniel McCarty, Gent., party thereto and a certificate of the execution thereof ordered to be recorded. Teste

Page 151.
Middleton to Middleton
This indenture made the 10th day of August 1771, between Alice Middleton and Leazure Middleton of the Parish of Washington and County of Westmoreland of the one part and Thomas Middleton of the same parish and county of the other part. Witnesseth that Alice Middleton and Leazure Middleton in consideration of 5 shillings as also for the natural love and affection and for other good causes and considerations have sold and released to the said Thomas Middleton a tenement and plantation with the full quantity of 25 acres of land adjoining whereon the said Thomas Middleton now lives, situate and being in the said Parish of Cople and County of Westmoreland being part of a tract of 150 acres which was formerly purchased by Matthew Harrison late of the County of Richmond, deceased of Alice Middleton first party to these presents and by the last will and testament of the said Matthew Harrison dated the 13th day of October 1764 demised to the said Alice Middleton and Leazure Middleton as tenants for life and after their death to be and remain to William Middleton and Thomas Middleton sons of the said Leazure Middleton in the fee simple. In witness whereof the parties to these presents have hereunto interchangeably set their hands and seals the day month and year above written.

Signed sealed and delivered in presence of us — Alice Middleton (her mark)
John Harrison, Jr. — Leazure Middleton (her mark)
Samuel Walker
Jeremiah Harrison, William Anderson
William Harrison
At a court held for Westmoreland County the 24th day of September 1771 this indenture and the receipt endorsed were proved by the oaths of Samuel Walker, Jeremiah Harrison, William Anderson and William Harrison witnesses thereto and ordered to be recorded. Teste

Page 154.
Robert Middleton's Will
In the name of God, Amen, by Robert Middleton of the County of Westmoreland and Parish of Cople do make this my last will and testament.
In the first place I desire all my just debts may be paid, then my will is that all my estate of whatever kind that is left may be kept together (until my youngest child comes to age of 16 years) for the use and benefit of my dear wife Elizabeth Middleton and my children so that my children may be supported at the discretion of my executors.
It is my will that on the arrival of my youngest child to the age of 16 that two thirds of my personal estate, such as negroes, stocks &c be equally divided among my children.
It is likewise my will and desire that my land (at the time of my youngest child comes to the age of 16) be sold and the money arising from it be equally divided among my children allowing my wife one third of the land during her life.
I do hereby appoint Mr. Thomas Fisher and Richard Lingan Hall my executors to this my last will. I witness whereof I have hereunto set my hand and seal this 26th day of February 1771.
In presence of — Robert Middleton
Ashton Lamkin
Thomas Chandler
Osmond Crabb (his mark)
At a court held for Westmoreland County the 24th day of September 1771 this will was proved according to law by the oaths of Thomas Chandler and Osmond Crabb witnesses thereto and ordered to be recorded. The executors therein named refused to take upon themselves the burden of the execution thereof.
Memorandum. At court held for the said County the 24th day of November 1771 on the motion of Daniel Tebbs and Daniel Bennett who made oath according to law and together with Edward Ransdell, Jr., and Peter Rust their securities entered into and acknowledged bond with condition as the law directs certificate is granted them for obtaining letters of administration of the estate of the said decedent with the will annexed in due form. Teste

Page 155.
Smith to Smith Indenture
This indenture made the 23rd day of September 1771 between Peter Smith, Sr., of Cople Parish and Westmoreland County of the one part and William Smith of the same parish and county, son of the said Peter Smith, Sr., of the other part. Witnesseth that Peter Smith, Sr., in consideration of the natural love and affection which he hath and for the better maintenance and livelihood has given and confirmed by these presents unto William Smith and his heirs and assigns forever all that tenement of land whereon he the said William Smith now liveth and has lived for several years past the bounds of which has been marked out by the said Peter Smith, Sr., and is supposed to contain about 35 acres, which said tract is part of the tract whereon the said Peter Smith, Sr., now liveth and joins the lands of Charles Carter, Esq. of Corotoman in the parish and county aforesaid. In witness whereof I the said Peter Smith, Sr., have hereunto set my hand and affixed my seal the day month and year above written.
Signed sealed and delivered in the presence of — Peter Smith, Sr. (his mark)

Joseph Lane, John Yeatman
Hugh Thomas, Jr.
At a court held for Westmoreland County the 24th day of September 1771 this deed of gift was proved by the oaths of Joseph Lane, John Yeatman and Hugh Thomas, Jr., the witnesses thereto and ordered to be recorded. Teste

Page 156.
Courtney to Smith Indenture
This indenture made the 20th day of June 1771 between Dorcas Courtney of the Parish of Cople and County of Westmoreland of the one part and Spence Smith of the County of Northumberland of the other part. Witnesseth that Dorcas Courtney in consideration of 5 pounds current money has sold unto Spence Smith all that tract of land which I now live on containing by estimation 143 acres, the land being on Potomack River and bounded by the land of Richard Lee, Daniel McCarty and Willoughby Newton. In witness whereof the parties above named have interchangeably set their hands and seals the day and year first above written.
Signed sealed and delivered in presence of
John Rust, Thomas Smith Garner
Samuel McCave, Mary Smith (her mark)
At a court held for Westmoreland County the 29th day of October 1771 this indenture was proved by the oaths of John Rust, Samuel McCave, and Thomas Smith Garner, witnesses thereto and ordered to be recorded. Teste

Page 157.
William McClanahan's Will
In the name of God, Amen, I William McClanahan of the County of Westmoreland and Parish of Cople being in perfect health and memory doth make and ordain this my last will and testament.
I lend to my beloved wife Martha McClanahan all my estate both real and personal during her natural life.
Item I lend to my son in law Garland Moore that tract of land whereon he now lives in Richmond County after my said wife's decease during his natural life and after his decease it is my will that the said land should be sold to the highest bidder and the money arising thereby to be equally divided between my five grandchildren, Robert Moore, Garland Moore, Peter Moore, McClanahan Moore and Martha Moore.
Item it is my will and desire that after the decease of my said wife Martha McClanahan that all my estate not mention both real and personal shall then be equally divided (by lots) between my five sons, Thomas McClanahan, Peter McClanahan, William McClanahan, James McClanahan, and John McClanahan and their heirs.
I do appoint Thomas McClanahan, Peter McClanahan and William McClanahan my whole and sole executors of this my last will and testament. In witness whereof I have hereunto set my hand and seal this 15th day of September 1760.
Peter Fleming — William McClanahan (his mark)
Edward Gill (his mark)
William Baley (his mark)
James Baley
Vincent S. Baley
At a court held for Westmoreland County the 29th day of October 1771 this will was proved according to law by the oath of Vincent S. Baley a witness thereto and the same having been before proved by the oath of James Baley another witness and ordered to be recorded and on the motion of Peter McClanahan one of the executors therein named who made oath thereto according to law and together with Thomas Edwards his security entered into and acknowledged bond with condition as the law directs, certificate is granted them for obtaining

a probate thereof in due form. Teste

Page 158.
<u>Neale & Wife to Gordan Indenture</u>
This indenture made this 4th day of Mary 1771 Between Richard Neale and Frances Neale his wife of the County of Westmoreland of the one part and John Gordon of the County of Richmond of the other part. Witnesseth that Richard Neale and Frances Neale his wife in consideration of 373 pounds 10 shillings lawful money of Virginia has sold to John Jordan a tract of land lying in the Parish of Cople and County of Westmoreland containing by estimation 110 acres, bounded as follows; beginning at a small red oak standing near a branch which divides this land from the land of William Stewart Minor and extending down branch to the Great Swamp and up the said swamp to the junction of the Spring Branch and up the Spring Branch to a gum thence South West 86 poles to a small red oak, the beginning. Purchased by the said William Black of John Spence and by the said Black and Frances his wife sold and conveyed to Alexander Spark, and by the said Alexander Spark and Elizabeth Spark his wife has sold and conveyed to the said Richard Neale.
The said Richard Neale and Frances Neale his wife for the same consideration before mentioned do likewise sell another small tract of land lying in the parish and county aforesaid containing by estimation 17 acres, be the same more or less beginning at a small gum tree standing by William Sturman's Spring Branch and running from thence along a row of marked trees, along the line of William Stewart Minor to a branch on which was formerly a mill which belong to Dr. William Flood and at this time belonging to John Turberville, and along the said branch to the junction of Sturman's Spring Branch, and up the said branch to the beginning place. In witness whereof, the said Richard Neale and Frances Neale his wife have hereunto set their hands and seals the day and year first above written.
Signed sealed and delivered in presence of Richard Neale
James Davenport Frances Neale
Hudson Muse
James Muse
Henry Fauntleroy
At a court held for Westmoreland County, the 29th day of October 1771, this indenture and receipt endorsed was acknowledged by Richard Neale and France Neale his wife (she being first privy examined as the law directs) parties thereto and ordered to be recorded.
Teste James Davenport CWC

County, Virginia Deeds & Wills 1768-1773; DB-15 {Abstract by Mike Marshall}; Page 161.
<u>Washington & Wife to Muse Indenture</u>
This indenture made the 24th day of November 1771 between John Augustine Washington and Hannah Washington his wife of the Parish of Cople and County of Washington of the one part and John Muse of the Parish of Washington and county aforesaid of the other part. Witnesseth that John Augustine Washington and Hannah Washington his wife in consideration of 500 pounds current money has sold to John Muse a tract of land with appurtenances lying in the Parish of Washington and County of Westmoreland containing by estimation 500 acres bounded on Mattox Creek, the lands of Nathaniel Washington, the lands late the property of Maximillian Robinson, and the lands belonging to the estate of James How, decd., which tract of land descended John Augustine Washington by the will of Augustine Washington, his father, bearing date the 11th day of April 1743. In witness whereof the parties have hereunto set their hands and seals the day and year above written.
Richard Lee John Augustine Washington
William Pierce Hannah Washington
Philip Smith
At a court held for Westmoreland County the 26th day of November 1771 this indenture and receipt endorsed were acknowledged by John Augustine Washington and Hannah

Washington his wife, parties thereto (she being first privy examined as the law directs, and ordered to be recorded. Teste

Page 162.
Rust to Rust Deed of Gift
I Samuel Rust of the County of Westmoreland in consideration of the natural love and affection which I have and beareth unto my son Peter Rust has given and confirmed unto him the land I bought of Samuel Eskridge, deceased, where Mrs. Jane Eskridge lives and the land that was James Courtney's where Mrs. Campbell and Jeremiah Courtney now lives with all it appurtenances and bounded as followeth; beginning at a bridge near Mrs. Elizabeth Rust's gate on a branch of Yeocomico River, thence along the said branch to the land of James Rust, thence along the said James Rust's line to the head of a cove on the aforesaid branch of Yeocomico River, thence down to the point, commonly called Knott's land from thence up Earle's Creek and a branch of the said creek to the road that leads into Yeocomico Neck, thence [xxxx] the said road to a small red oak a corner tree to George Rust's land, from thence along the lines of the said George Rust and Capt. Peter Rust's heirs, to the beginning all within the aforesaid bounds contains by estimation 378 acres. In witness whereof I have set my hand and seal this 26th day of November 1771.
Signed sealed and delivered in presents of Samuel Rust
Hugh Hamilton
Daniel Bennett
Robert Jeffries
At a court held for Westmoreland County, the 26th day of November 1771, This indenture was acknowledged by Samuel Rust party thereto and ordered to be recorded. Teste

Page 163.
Rust & Wife to Rust Indenture
This indenture made the 26th day of November 1771 between Peter Rust of the Parish of Cople and County of Westmoreland of the one part and Samuel Rust of the parish and county aforesaid of the other part. Witnesseth that Peter Rust and Rebecca Rust his wife in consideration of 150 pounds current money and for other good causes and considerations, him thereunto moving has sold unto Samuel Rust all the land & appurtenances thereunto belonging that he now lives on, lying in the parish and county aforesaid by estimation 175 acres and bounded as followeth; beginning at a stone that formerly was Jeffries corner, from thence Northeasterly to a white oak standing by the Warehouse Road, from thence along the line of Tebbs and Bailey to Marsh Cove and down the said cove to the creek neck and up the said creek and branch to the beginning stone. In Witness whereof he the said Peter Rust and Rebecca Rust his wife hath hereunto set their hands and seals the day and year above written.
Signed sealed and delivered in presence of Peter Rust
Hugh Hamilton Rebecca Rust
Daniel Bennett, Robert Jeffries
At a court held Westmoreland County the 24th day of November 1771, this indenture of feoffment together with the memorandum of livery of seizen and receipt endorsed were acknowledged by Peter Rust party thereto and ordered to be recorded.

Page 165.
Joseph Stone's Will
In the name of God, Amen, the 16th day of December 1770, I Joseph Stone of the Parish of Cople and County of Westmoreland being in a low state of health but of a perfect memory do here make my last will and testament in the following manner and form.
Item give and bequeath unto my son Thomas Stone my land I now live on and Negro man Dick, and five shillings sterling.

Item I give and bequeath unto my wife Ann Stone, Negro man Old Jack [during] her life and then to return to my other children.
Item I give and bequeath unto my two children, Presley Stone and the child my wife Ann Stone is with child with, two Negroes, Young Jack and Moll, to be equally divided between them when my son Presley Stone arrives at age. But my will is that my wife have the use of the two negroes till they come of age.
Item I give and bequeath unto my daughter Jemima Neale, Negro boy Natt which I gave her when she was married, and Negro boy Bob.
Item I give and bequeath unto my daughter Penelope Stone, Negro woman Jenny, and further my will and desire that my wife and other children give her out of their parts two pounds apiece paid to her when she is at age.
Item That my two tracts of leased land be sold for the use of my wife and children and what of my estate not mentioned be equally divided amongst them all.
Lastly, I appoint my wife Ann Stone, Thomas Stone and Rodham Neale to be my executors.
As witness whereof I have hereunto set my hand and seal in the year of our Lord 1770.
Signed sealed in the presence of us Joseph Stone
Youell Sanford
William Brawner
James Moore
Rodham Neale
At a court held for Westmoreland County the 24th day of November 1771 this will was produced in pursuance of a former order of this court and being proved by the oaths of Youell Sanford, William Brawner, and James Moore, witnesses thereto is ordered to be recorded and on the motion of Rodham Neale one of the executors therein named who made oath thereto according to law and together with James Muse and Thomas Stone his securities entered into and acknowledged bond with condition as the law directs, certificate is granted him for obtaining a probate thereof in due form. Previous to which, Ann Stone, the widow and executrix in the said will named, personally appeared and renounced all benefit and advantage claim under the said will. Teste

Page 167.
Hamrick & Wife to McKenney Indenture
This indenture made this 21st day of July 1769 between Isaac Hamrick and Hannah Hamrick his wife of the Parish of Dettingen and County of Prince William, planter of the one part and John McKenney of the County of Westmoreland and Parish of Cople of the other part. Witnesseth that Isaac Hamrick and Hannah Hamrick his wife in consideration of 20 pounds current money and sold to John McKenney have sold a tract of land containing 50 acres lying in the Parish of Cople and County of Westmorland being part of a tract of land whereon Samuel Garner formerly lived and was left to the said Hannah Hamrick by the last will and testament of her deceased father George Halcom [Haughlcom], which said land adjoins the land of Henry Asbury, deceased. In witness whereof the said Isaac Hamrick and Hannah Hamrick his wife have hereunto set their hands and seals the day and year above written.
Sealed signed and delivered in presence of Isaac Hamrick
Richard Lee, Joseph Lane, Jr. Hannah Hamrick (her mark)
James Lane, Jeremiah Cockerill
John Wake, William Lane, Jr.
Charles Clark
William Carr Lane, Jonathan Wilson
To James Lane, William Carr Lane and George Summers, of the County of Loudoun, greeting. Whereas Isaac Hamrick and Hannah Hamrick his wife by their indenture of bargain and sale bearing date the 27th day of July have sold and conveyed unto John McKenney the fee simple estate 50 acres of land lying in the Parish of Cople and County of Westmoreland, and whereas the said Hannah Hamrick cannot conveniently travel to her court of our said

County to make acknowledgment. Therefore, we do give unto you or any two of you power to receive the acknowledgment which the said Hannah shall be willing to make. Witness James Davenport, clerk of our said court the 13th day of April 1769.
By virtue of the above writ to us directed we did personally go to the said Hannah Hamrick the wife of the above-named Isaac Hamrick and before us she did acknowledge the indenture hereunder annexed to be her act and deed and that she did the same freely and voluntarily without the persuasions or threats of her husband and was willing that the same should be recorded in the County Court of Westmoreland. All which we certify under our hands and seals this 29th day of July 1769.
James Lane
William Carr Lane
At a court held for Westmoreland County the 26th day of November 1771 this indenture of feoffment with the memorandum of livery of seizen and receipt thereon endorsed were proved by the oath of Charles Clark one of the witnesses thereto and the same having been before proved by two other the witnesses thereto are together with the commission annexed for taking the acknowledgment and privy examination of Hannah Hamrick the wife of Isaac Hamrick party thereto and a certificate of the execution thereof ordered to be recorded. Teste

Page 171.
John Moxley's Will
In the name of God, Amen, I John Moxley of Washington Parish and the County of Westmoreland being weak in body but of sound and perfect memory do make this my last will and testament in manner and form as followeth.
Item I give and bequeath to my dear beloved wife Elizabeth Moxley all my stock of horses, cattle and hogs, and household furniture where I now live, only my mare which I do give to my son Augustine Moxley, but all the rest I give to my said wife and her heirs forever.
Item I give and bequeath to my son Augustine Moxley all my stock of cattle, horses, hogs and sheep, and all the household furniture where he now lives, excepting one young cow and calf which I do give to my loving wife, all the rest I give to my said son and his heirs forever.
Lastly, I do appoint and ordain my dear beloved wife Elizabeth Moxley and my son Augustine Moxley, whole and sole executrix and executors of this my last will and testament. In confirmation whereof I have hereunto set my hand and affixed my seal the 14th day of August 1771.
Signed sealed and delivered in presence of us John Moxley (his mark)
Augustine Sanford
Robert Sanford, Jr.
At a court held for Westmoreland County the 26th day of November 1771 this will was proved according to law by the oaths of Augustine Sanford and Robert Sanford, Jr., the witnesses thereto and ordered to be recorded and on the motion of Augustine Moxley the executor therein named who made oath thereto according to law and together with Willoughby Sanford and Joseph Moxley his securities entered into and acknowledged bond with condition as the law directs, certificate is granted him for obtaining a probate thereof in due form. Teste

Page 172.
Smith & Wife to Yeatman Indenture
This indenture made 26th day of November 1771 between Peter Smith, Jr., and Sarah Smith his wife of Cople Parish and County of Westmoreland of the one part and John Yeatman of the same Parish and County of the other part. Whereas John Baker of the Parish of Cople and County of Westmoreland by his last will and testament bearing date the third day of September 1748 devised to his son William Baker a tract of land lying on one of the branches of Nominy containing by estimation 50 acres and bounded by the lands of Dunkin and Remy (now Rochester), White, and the said John Yeatman and Porter, and the said William Baker died without a will and left only two daughters, Sarah Baker and Susanna

Baker who are coheirs and married with the said Peter Smith, Jr., and the said John Yeatman parties to these presents who have made no division of the same. Now this indenture witnesseth that the said Peter Smith, Jr., and Sarah Smith his wife in consideration of 15 pounds current money of Virginia have sold unto John Yeatman all other part of the above-mentioned tract of land being 25 acres which is one half of the said tract of 50 acres. In witness whereof the parties to these presents have interchangeably set their hands and seals the day month and year first above written.

Signed sealed and delivered in presence of Peter Smith
Sarah Smith

At a court held for Westmoreland County the 26th day of November 1771 this indenture and receipt endorsed were acknowledged by Peter Smith, Jr., and Sarah Smith his wife parties thereto (she being first privily examined as the law directs) and ordered to be recorded. Teste

Page 175.

Samuel Stowers' Will

In the name of God Amen, I Samuel Stowers of Cople Parish and County of Westmoreland, planter being sound and disposing mind and memory do make and ordain this my last will and testament.

Item I give and bequeath to my cousin Samuel Stowers of the county aforesaid half of my estate.

Item I do give unto Ann Stowers my loving wife, the other half during her life and after her departure to fall to my said cousin Samuel Stowers.

Lastly, I do make and constitute Ann Stowers, my said wife executrix of this my last will and testament dated this 24th day of December 1762.

Sealed and delivered in the presence of Samuel Stowers (his mark)
Thomas Newman
William Fryer
William Jackson

At a court held for Westmoreland County 31st day of October 1771 this will having been proved accordingly to law in August last by the oath of William Jackson a witness thereto and being now again presented to the Court by Samuel Stowers is ordered to be recorded for reasons appearing to the court and on the motion of the said Samuel Stowers who made oath thereto according to law together with Thomas Atwell his security entered into and acknowledged bond with condition as the law directs certificate is granted him for obtaining letters of the administration of the estate of the testator with the said will and next in due form. Teste

County, Virginia Deeds & Wills 1768-1773; DB-15 {Abstract by Mike Marshall}; Page 176.

John Bulger's Will

In the name of God, Amen, the 23rd day of December 1771 I John Bulger of the County of Westmoreland being sick and weak in body but of perfect mind and memory do make and ordain this my last will and testament.

All my stock of all kinds shall be sold for a 12-month credit, corn and all my household furniture.

Further it is my will and desire that all my Negroes should be rented out to the highest bidder until all my just debts be paid. Also, my lease to be sold to the highest bidder.

I give and bequeath to my daughter Barbery Jenkins, Negro wench Silvey.

I give to my daughter Elizabeth Parsons, Negro man Tom.

I give to my son Johnson Bulger, Negro girl Hannah.

I give to my daughter Sally Bulger, Negro man Essex.

I give to my daughter Nancy Bulger, Negro boy Daniel.

Lastly, I appoint Mr. Thomas Jett executor of this my last will and testament. In witness

whereof I have hereunto set my hand and seal the day and date above written.
Signed sealed in the presence of John Bulger
John Omohundro
Richard Muse
John Washington, Jr. (his mark)
At a court held for Westmoreland County to 31st day of December 1771 this will was proved according to law by the oaths of Richard Muse and John Washington, Jr., witnesses thereto and ordered to be recorded and on the motion of Thomas Jett executor therein named who made oath thereto according to law and together with the said Richard Muse and George Newman his securities entered into and acknowledged bond with condition that if the law directs, certificate is granted him for obtaining a probate thereof in due form. Teste

Page 177.
John Brown's Will
In the name of God, Amen, the 14th day of May 1770 I John Brown of the County of Westmoreland being very sick and weak of body but of perfect mind and memory do make and ordain this my last will and testament.
Item I give unto my son William Brown the land that fell to me by the death of William Fryer, deceased to him and his heirs.
Item I give to my son William Brown, Negro man Jack, and all the stock and household furniture that he has in possession that came by the death of William Fryer, deceased.
Item I give to my son John Brown the plantation and tract of land that I now live on and likewise the land I bought of George Duren, Negro girl Rose, Negro boy Daniel, one feather bed and furniture, the best I have, one grey breeding mare, one sorrel horse with a blaze face, four cows and calves of his choice, one desk I bought at Porter's sale, the largest all full table and the largest looking glass.
Item I give to my daughter Priscilla Brown, Negro man Adam, Negro boy Orange, one feather bed and furniture, the second choice.
I leave the land whereon Wittington McKenney now lives to be sold to pay debts.
I leave unto my son John Brown and my seven daughters that is now living the remainder of my estate which consists of slaves, stocks and household furniture and all debts due to me to be equally divided amongst them after my debts being paid first. I leave William Brown and my son John Brown my executors. Signed and acknowledge in presence of us.
Gerard Hutt John Brown
William Robinson Dozier
At a court held for Westmoreland County the 31st day of December 1771 this will was proved according to law by the oaths of Gerard Hutt and William Robinson Dozier the witnesses thereto and ordered to be recorded and on the motion of William Brown one of the executors therein named who made oath thereto according to law and together with Gerard Hutt and William Robinson Dozier his securities entered into and acknowledged bond with condition as the law directs, certificate is granted him for obtaining a probate thereof in due form; liberty being reserve to John Brown the other executor therein named to join in the probate thereof when he shall think fit. Teste

Page 179.
Henry Cavender's Will
In the name of God, Amen, I Henry Cavender of Cople Parish in County of Westmoreland being very sick and weak do make and ordain this my last will and testament.
Item I give and bequeath to my daughter Ann Davis, one shilling sterling and cut her off from having any other right to any part of my estate.
Item I leave to my loving wife Elizabeth Cavender all my estate both real and personal during her natural life and after her decease as followeth.
Item I give and bequeath to my son Thomas Cavender the bed stead and furniture that is

now in the tobacco house to be delivered to him immediately and four head of cattle after the decease of my wife.
Item I give and bequeath to my son John Cavender the bed stead and furniture I now lye on and four head of cattle and my young mare.
Item I give and bequeath to my daughter Rachel Nash my other bedstead and furniture that is now upstairs, one cow and calf and side saddle.
It is my will and desire that all the rest of my estate after the decease of my wife, shall be equally divided amongst my three last mentioned children and my son George Cavender.
I leave my loving wife Elizabeth Cavender and my son George Cavender my whole and sole executors of this my last will and testament, December 24, 1771
Signed sealed and delivered in presence of us Henry Cavender (his mark)
Thomas Edwards
George Sanford
Sarah Sturman (her mark)
John McGuire (his mark)
At a court held for Westmoreland County the 31st day of March 1772 this will was proved according to law by the oaths of Thomas Edwards and George Sanford witnesses thereto and ordered to be recorded and on the motion of George Cavender one of the executors therein named who made oath thereto according to law and together with the said Thomas Edwards his security entered into and acknowledged bond with the condition as the law directs, certificate is granted him for obtaining a probate thereof in due form. Teste

Page 180.
Mary Read's Will
In the name of God, Amen, I Mary Read of the County of Westmoreland, spinster, being sick and weak but of sound and disposing mind and memory do make this my last will and testament in manner and form following.
First, I give and devise to my sister Ann Asbury four slaves: Will, Lucy, Dinah and Nan, also the bed and furniture that is at her house.
Item I give and bequeath to my niece Barbary Hutt all my wearing apparel.
I give the five following slaves; Peter, Dick, Dacus, Judy and Sinah and all the rest and residue of my estate both real and personal to my nephew Andrew Read for and during his natural life and after his decease to my godson Joseph Read son of the said Andrew Read.
I do hereby charge the said estate to devise to the said Andrew Read with 5 pounds annually to be laid out in the purchase of clothes for my brother Richard Read during his natural life, a hat only to be purchased this present year he being in every other respect clothed and I do charge the said estate with the education of my said godson Joseph Read.
Lastly, I do constitute my said sister Ann Asbury and my nephew Andrew Read executors of this my last will and testament.
In testimony whereof I have hereunto set my hand and seal this 21st day of January 1772
Signed sealed and acknowledged in presence of us Mary Read (her mark)
Richard Parker
Thomas Asbury
At a court held for Westmoreland County the 31st day of March 1772 this will was proved according to law by the oaths of Richard Parker and Thomas Asbury the witnesses thereto and ordered to be recorded and on the motion of Ann Asbury and Andrew Read the executors therein named who made oath thereto according to law and together with John Lawson their security entered into and acknowledged bond with condition as the law directs, certificate is granted them for obtaining a probate thereof in due form.
Teste James Davenport CWC

Page 181.
Moxley to Wife Deed of Trust & Gift

I Richard Moxley, Jr., of the County of Westmoreland for the entire love and affection which I have and do bear to my loving wife and children, I do give the following slaves and others estate (to wit) I do give my trusty friends, Daniel Muse, Richard Moxley, Hudson Muse, and Daniel Muse, Jr. my four Negroes; George, Betty, Adam, and Beck in trust nevertheless for the use and benefit of my loving wife for and during her natural life and after her decease the said Negroes and all their future increase I give to be equally divided between all my children which I have or she may bear by me;
I give to my daughter Molly Moxley, Negro woman Betty Permudas and her increase.
I give to my son Daniel Moxley, my two Negro boys; Ephraim and Charles.
I give to my son Richard Moxley an equal part of my whole estate.
I give to my daughter Hannah Dozier Moxley, one equal part of my whole personal estate.
I give to my daughter Betsy Muse Moxley, Negro girl Lydia and her increase, also an equal part of the rest of my personal estate which she is not herein before given, and all the rest of my whole personal estate which I have not already given I give to my trusty friends in behalf of my wife above mentioned in all my children which I have or may have by my wife during our natural lives the same to be equally divided between them. In witness whereof I have hereunto set my hand and seal the 18th day of January 1772.
Sealed and delivered in presence of us Richard Moxley, Jr.
Augustine Sanford
Richard Neale
Thomas Yeatman
Memorandum; I give to my daughter Hannah Dozier Moxley, Negro girl Peggy which I did not mention and her increase. In confirmation whereof I have hereunto set my hand and seal this 18th day of January 1772.
Sealed and delivered in presence of us Richard Moxley, Jr.
Augustine Sanford
Richard Neale
Thomas Yeatman
At a court held for Westmoreland County the 31st day of March 1772 this deed of gift was proved by the oaths of Augustine Sanford and Richard Neale witnesses thereto and ordered to be recorded.
Teste James Davenport CWC

Page 182.
Tebbs & Wife to Ballantine Privy Examination
To Richard Henry Lee, Richard Lee and George Turberville of the County of Westmoreland. Whereas Daniel Tebbs and Elizabeth Tebbs his wife of the County of Westmoreland by their indenture of bargain and sale bearing date the ninth day of December 1769 hath conveyed unto John Ballantine, Sr., of the aforesaid county the fee simple estate of 460 acres lying in the Parish of Cople and County aforesaid and whereas the said Elizabeth cannot conveniently travel to record to make acknowledgment. Therefore, we do give unto you or any two of you power to receive the acknowledgment which the said Elizabeth Tebbs shall be willing to make. Witness James Davenport, clerk of our said court the seventh day of August 1771.
Westmoreland Sct. We whose names are hereunto subscribed and seals affixed have in obedience to the writ hereunder annexed examined Mrs. Elizabeth Tebbs (wife of Daniel Tebbs both of this County) privately and apart from her husband and find her consenting freely and voluntarily without the persuasion or threats of her husband to an indenture of bargain and sale conveyance unto John Ballantine, Sr., the fee simple estate of 460 acres of land by and in the Parish of Cople and County aforesaid and that she is willing the said indenture shall be recorded in the County Court. Given under our hands and seals the 30th day of August 1771.
Richard Henry Lee

George Turberville
At a court continued and held for Westmoreland County the first day of April 1772 this commission for the privy examination of Elizabeth the wife of Daniel Tebbs and a certificate of the execution thereof being returned are ordered to be recorded.
Teste James Davenport CWC

Page 184.
Thomas Monroe's Will
In the name of God, Amen, I Thomas Monroe of the County of Westmoreland being weak but of disposing since and memory do make constitute and ordain this my last will and testament.
Imprimis, I give and devise to my brother Andrew Monroe, Negro James, of the 10 pounds cash out of him to be paid to my brother James Monroe.
Item I give and devise to my sister Martha Monroe, one bay mare and 8 pounds cash to pay for a saddle.
Item I give and devise to my sister Jane Monroe, 40 shillings cash.
Item I give and devise to my sister Martha Monroe the rest of my estate to buy her clothes.
Lastly, I appoint my brother Andrew Monroe my executor of this my last will and testament. In testimony whereof I hereunto set my hand and seal this ninth day of March 1772.
In presence of Thomas Monroe
Andrew Monroe
George Weedon
At a court held for Westmoreland County the 28th day of April 1772 this will was proved according to law by the oaths of Andrew Monroe and George Weedon the witnesses thereto and ordered to be recorded and on the motion of Andrew Monroe, Jr., the executor therein named who made oath thereto according to law and together with Rachel Monroe his security entered into and acknowledged by with the condition as the law directs, certificate is granted him for obtaining a probate thereof in due form.
Teste James Davenport CWC

Page 185.
Alice Middleton's Will
In the name of God, Amen, the 27th day of October 1766 by Alice Middleton of the County of Westmoreland and Parish of Cople and Colony of Virginia being sick and weak of body but of perfect mind and memory do make constitute ordain and declare this my last will and testament in manner and form following.
Item I give and bequeath and to Thomas Middleton, son of Thomas Middleton, deceased, one feather bed and furniture, and one bell metal skillet.
Item I give and bequeath all my other estate movable and immovable to be equally divided between William Middleton and Thomas Middleton, sons of the aforesaid Thomas Middleton, deceased.
Item I nominate, ordain and appoint Samuel Walker and the above-mentioned William Middleton whole and sole executors of this my last will and testament. In witness whereof I have hereunto set my hand and seal the day and year above written.
Signed sealed published and pressure of Alice Middleton
Smith King, William Rust
John Middleton, William Harrison
At a court held for Westmoreland County the 28th day of April 1772 this will was proved according to law by the oath of Smith King a witness thereto and ordered to be recorded and on motion of Samuel Walker and William Middleton the executors therein named who made oath thereto according to law and together with the said Smith King their security entered into and acknowledged bond with condition as the law directs, certificate is granted them for obtaining a probate thereof in due form.

Teste James Davenport CWC

Page 186.
Jane Muse Renunciation of Husband's Will
know all men by these presents that I Jane Muse of the Parish of Washington in County of Westmoreland, widow of John Muse, heretofore of the same parish and county. Whereas the said John Muse was in his lifetime and at his death seized and possessed of a very considerable estate real and personal and being so seized and possessed of the said estate duly made his last will and testament in writing and died sometime in the month of January last past without altering or revoking the said will and whereas I the said Jane Muse have reason to believe and apprehend that the said John Muse hath not made an adequate or equitable provision in and by this said will or his last will for me, the said Jane Muse. Now this indenture witnesseth that I the said Jane Muse do declare that I will not accept, receive or take the legacy or legacies to me given and bequeathed or any part thereof and that I have and hereby do renounce all benefit and advantages which I might claim by the said last will of the said John Muse and I the said Jane Muse have and hereby do execute this indenture to entitle me the said Jane to demand and receive my dower in the estate of the said John Muse according to law. In witness whereof I the said Jane Muse have hereunto set my hand and seal this 27th day of April 1772.
Signed sealed and acknowledged in presence of Jane Muse
John Martin
Hugh Lietch
William Nelson
At a court held for Westmoreland County the 28th day of April 1772 this deed poll of renunciation of the will of John Muse, deceased was proved by the oaths of John Martin, Hugh Lietch and William Nelson the witnesses there and ordered to be recorded.
Teste James Davenport CWC

Page 187.
Asbury & Wife to Edwards Indenture
This indenture made the 28th day of April 1772 between Ann Asbury, widow of the late, deceased Thomas Asbury and Henry Asbury, son and heir and Ann Asbury his wife of the Parish of Lunenburg and County of Richmond of the one part and Thomas Edwards of the Parish of Cople and County of Westmoreland of the other part. Whereas the aforesaid Ann Asbury and Henry Asbury and Ann Asbury his wife being heirs of two tracts of land containing 180 acres lying in the forest of Nominy in Cople Parish and County of Westmoreland 100 acres the plantation Ann Davis lives, formerly the property of Benjamin Asbury, known by the name of Talbutts, the other 80 acres being formerly the property of the said Benjamin Asbury known by the name of Dowsitts. Now this indenture witnesseth that Ann Asbury and Henry Asbury and Ann Asbury his wife in consideration of 90 pounds current money of Virginia has sold to Thomas Edwards the aforesaid 180 acres with all appurtenances. In witness whereof the said Ann Asbury and Henry Asbury and Ann Asbury his wife have hereunto set their hands and seals this 28th day of April 1772.
NB. One acre is excepted out of this deed being the place where the said Henry Asbury ancestors were buried.
Signed sealed and delivered in presence of us Ann Asbury
Alexander Spark Henry Asbury
Daniel Tebbs Ann Asbury
Thomas Atwell
William Brown
At a court held for Westmoreland County the 28th day of April 1772 the foregoing indenture and bond for the performance of covenants together with a receipt on the said indenture endorsed were proved by the oaths of Alexander Spark, Daniel Tebbs, Thomas Atwell and

William Brown the witnesses thereto and ordered to be recorded, previous to which Ann Asbury wife of Henry Asbury, party thereto being first privy examined as the law directs, voluntarily relinquished her right of dower in the estate conveyed by the said indenture.
Teste James Davenport CWC

Page 191.
John Smith's Will
In the name of God, Amen, I John Smith, Gent., of the County of Westmoreland do make this my last will and testament.
I give and bequeath to my three sons, John Smith, Edward Smith and Matthew Smith all my estate both real and personal and mixed to them and their heirs to be equally divided.
I constitute and appoint my three sons to be executors to this my last will. In witness whereof I have hereunto set my hand and seal the 7th day of January 1771.
Signed sealed published in the presence of us John Smith
Richard Buckner
Philip Smith
John Lee
At a court held for Westmoreland County the 28th day of April 1772, this will was proved according to law by the oaths of Philip Smith and John Lee, witnesses thereto and ordered to be recorded.
Teste James Davenport CWC

Page 192.
Rochester & Wife to Tidwell Indenture
This indenture made the 28th day of April 1772 between John Rochester and Ann Rochester his wife of the Parish of Cople and County of Westmoreland of the one part and William Carr Tidwell of the same parish and county of the other part. Witnesseth that John Rochester and Ann Rochester his wife in consideration of 120 pounds current money of Virginia has sold unto William Carr Tidwell all that parcel, dividend or tract of land lying on the lower side of Potter's Creek in the Parish of Cople and County of Westmoreland containing by estimation 114 acres and bounded as followeth. Beginning at a white oak standing on a point on Potter's Creek corner to the land where John McCullock, deceased lived, thence up the said creek and coves the several courses and meanders thereof to a large gum tree standing on the west side of a branch that runs into the said creek, thence South 26° West 38 pole to a stake on a level, thence along the crooked line of marked trees South 51° East 90 pole to three white oaks supposed to be the corner mentioned in James Thomas' survey, thence North 40° East 5 pole to a large pine, and small red oak, thence North 70° East 173 pole to a pine a corner of the said William Carr Tidwell, thence North East to a large red oak another corner to the same, thence North 56° East 16 Pole to a stake at the waterside, thence along the said water 12 pole to a swamp of gum tree another corner, to the said John McCullock and thence along his line to the beginning; which said land lies within the bounds and is part of a patent bearing date the 28th day of March 1662 for 500 acres first granted to Isaac Allerton, Gent., deceased and he gave and devised the same to his son Capt. Isaac Allerton, deceased, who sold and conveyed the same to Gerard Davis, deceased and he sold and conveyed the same to William Rochester, deceased who gave and devised the same to his son John Rochester, deceased who died intestate and then the same descended to and became vested in his eldest son John Rochester party to these presents. In witness whereof the parties above mentioned have hereunto interchangeably set their hands and affixed their seals the day month and year first above written.
Signed sealed and delivered in the presence of John Rochester
Ann Rochester
At a court held for Westmoreland County the 28th day of April 1772 the foregoing indenture and bond for performance of covenants together with the receipt on the said indenture

endorsed were acknowledged by John Rochester and Ann Rochester his wife parties thereto (she being first privy examined as the law directs and ordered to be recorded.
Teste James Davenport CWC

Page 195.
Lee to Atwell Indenture
this indenture made this 18th day of November 1771 between Richard Lee, Esq. of the one part and Thomas Atwell, planter of the other part. Witnesseth that the said Richard Lee in consideration of the rents and covenants herein after reserved has demised and to farm let unto the said Thomas Atwell the tenement of land in the tenure and occupation of the said Richard Lee lying in the County of Westmoreland and Parish of Cople commonly called and known by the name of Murphy's which said land Richard Lee purchased of John Murphy. To have and to hold the said tenement of 200 acres of land unto Thomas Atwell from the day of the date hereof for and during the natural lives of him the said Thomas Atwell and his son Thomas Atwell and the longest liver of them yielding and paying unto the said Richard Lee yearly and every year the rent of 2000 pounds of crop tobacco and cask, also the quit rents and any taxes that may be upon the land. And the said Thomas Atwell agrees with the said Richard Lee that he will leave standing in some convenient part of the above premises one body of at least 50 acres of woods untouched which shall remain and be held as a future support of the plantation, and further agrees within the space of one year to build on some convenient part of the land a dwelling house 20' x 16', a 40 foot tobacco house or corn house or other houses and buildings equal thereto, and also within the space of one year plant 100 winter apple trees at 30 feet distance every way from each other and 200 peach trees at 70 feet distance each way. In witness whereof the said parties have hereunto interchangeably set their hands and fixed their seals the day month and year first above written.
Signed sealed and delivered in the presence of Richard Lee
Benjamin Middleton Thomas Atwell
William Porter
Reuben Jordan
At a court held for Westmoreland County the 28th day of April 1772 this indenture of lease was acknowledged by Richard Lee and Thomas Atwell the parties thereto and ordered to be recorded.
Teste James Davenport CWC

Page 200.
Youell Holland's Will
In the name of God, Amen, I Youell Holland of the County of Westmoreland and Parish of Cople do make this my last will and testament.
I give unto my wife Hannah Holland one third of the land whereon I now live forever.
Item I will and bequeath to my daughter Rocky Holland two thirds of the land where he now lives to her and her heirs forever.
Item I will and bequeath unto my loving wife one bed and bedstead and furniture during her natural life and no longer.
Item I give unto my loving wife Hannah Holland one desk and one brass trunk during her natural life and no longer.
Item I give unto my daughter Rocky Holland one red Spanish trunk.
Item I give unto my loving wife Hannah Holland one common prayer book.
Item I give unto my daughter Rocky Holland one Holy Bible.
Item that it is my desire that my wife Hannah Holland have so much corn out of my crop as well serve her this next ensuing year and the rest be sold to the highest bidder for ready money.
Item it is my desire that all my fodder and tobacco, my hogs, my cattle and my horse and saddle and bridle, my ox chain and one plow and all my household furniture, that is not

before mentioned in this will shall be sold to the highest bidder and if so be there is more than will pay my debts, the third of it is to go to my wife Hannah Holland and the remaining part to my daughter Rocky Holland.

I do appoint my two friends John Brinnon and Thomas Welch my two executors. Given under my hand and seal 7th day of December 1771

Teste Youell Holland

Thomas Welch

John Brinnon, Jr.

Matthew Welch

At a court held for Westmoreland County the 26th day of May 1772 this will was proved according to law by the oaths of Thomas Welch and Matthew Welch witnesses thereto and ordered to be recorded and on the motion of John Brinnon one of the executors therein named who made oath thereto according to law and together with Solomon Robinson his security entered into and acknowledged upon with condition as the law directs, certificate is granted him for obtaining a probate thereof in due form. Memorandum Thomas Welch the other executor in the said will named personally appeared and refused to take upon himself the burthen of the execution thereof.

Test James Davenport CWC

Page 201.

Bailey to Bailey Indenture

This indenture made the 26th day of May 1772 between Jeremiah Garland Bailey of Cople Parish in Westmoreland County, planter of the one part and John Bailey of Westmoreland County and Parish of Washington, planter of the other part. Witnesseth that Jeremiah Garland Bailey in consideration of 60 pounds lawful money of Virginia already paid and for other good causes and consideration him thereunto moving has sold unto John Bailey all that tract of land containing 75 acres lying in the Parish of Washington and County of Westmoreland and bounded as follows; beginning at a white oak corner to the said Jeremiah Garland Bailey in the said John Bailey in Capt. James Blair's line, thence along the said John Bailey's line to Starks line, thence along the said Stark's line to a red oak corner to Stark in Moses Pittman's line to a corner to the said John Bailey in the said Pittman's line, thence along the said John Bailey's line to a spanish oak corner to the said John Bailey, the said Jeremiah Garland Bailey and the said James Blair's, thence along the said Blair's line to the beginning. In witness whereof the said Jeremiah Garland Bailey hath to this present indenture set his hand and affixed his seal the day and year first above written.

Signed sealed and delivered in the presence of us Jeremiah G. Bailey

At a court held for Westmoreland County the 26th day of May 1772 this indenture and receipt thereon endorsed were acknowledged by Jeremiah Garland Bailey, party thereto and ordered to be recorded.

Teste James Davenport Clk Cur

Page 203.

Washington to Anton Indenture

This indenture made the 26th day of May 1772 between Thomas Washington of the Parish of Cople and County of Westmoreland, planter of the one part and Alexander Anton of the parish and county aforesaid, weaver of the other part. Witnessed that Thomas Washington in consideration of the yearly rent, hereafter mentioned hath demised and to farm let unto Alexander Anton, Mary Anton and Robert Anton during their natural lives, one tenement and tract of land lying in the Parish of Cople and County of Westmoreland containing 69 acres and bounded as followeth; beginning at a red oak corner to the said Thomas Washington and Richard Moxley, thence to the crossroads which is a corner to Thomas Chilton's Gent., then along the road to the line of Thomas Omohundro's, so along the said Omohundro's line to the swamp, thence down the swamp to the mouth of a branch, so up the said branch to the beginning. To have and to hold during the term in space of natural lives of the said Alexander Anton, Mary Anton and Robert Anton or the longest liver yielding and paying every year during the said term, 3 pounds six shillings current money of Virginia on the first day of January and shall plant 150 peach trees and 25 apple trees upon the said premises under a good and lawful fence. In witness whereof the parties to these presents have hereunto interchangeably that their hands and seals the day month and year first above written. The first rent is payable the first day January 1774.

Signed sealed and delivered in the presence of us — Thomas Washington
Augustine Sanford — Alexander Anton

At a court held for Westmoreland County the 26th day of May 1772 this indenture of lease was acknowledged by Thomas Washington and Alexander Anton parties thereto and ordered to be recorded. Teste

Page 205.

Self to Morton Indenture

Indenture made the 30th day of December 1771 between Henry Self, Sr., of Cople Parish and County of Westmoreland of the one part and William Morton of the same parish and county of the other. Witnessed that Henry Self., Sr., in consideration of 30 pounds current money of Virginia has sold unto William Morton all that tract of land lying in the Parish of Cople in County of Westmoreland containing by estimation 64 acres which said land was given by Willoughby Harrison, deceased, to his son Samuel Harrison, as by his last will and testament, and the said Samuel Harrison sold the same to Henry Self, Sr., party to these presents as by deed of feoffment bearing date the 2nd day of March 1754, and bounded on the lands of Edmond Walker, deceased, and land formerly George Lamkin's. In witness whereof the parties first to these presents have interchangeably set his hand and seal the day month and year first above written. Henry Self

Signed sealed and delivered in presence of
Richard Lowe, Jr., William Jarvis Kendrick
William Danks, John Middleton

At a court held for Westmoreland County the 26th day of May 1772 this indenture and receipt endorsed were acknowledged by Henry Self party thereto and ordered to be recorded. Teste

Page 207.

Bailey to McClanahan Indenture

This indenture made the 21st day of October 1765 between John Bailey, son of William Bailey and William Bailey, Sr., father of the said John Bailey and Elizabeth Bailey, wife of the said John Bailey, of the County of Westmoreland and Parish of Cople of the one part and Peter McClanahan the same parish and county aforesaid of the other part. Witnesseth that John Bailey and Elizabeth Bailey his wife and William Bailey in consideration of 75 pounds current money has sold to Peter McClanahan all that parcel of land (except a burying place 30 ft.^{2}) situated and lying in the aforesaid County of Westmoreland and binding on the land of the Hon. Robert Carter, Esq. and on the land of the aforesaid Peter McClanahan, containing by estimation 75 acres, which said land was the property of Elizabeth Bailey, mother of the said John Bailey and descended to the said John Bailey has been heir at law. In witness whereof the parties to these presents hath interchangeably set their hands and fixed their seals the day and year above written.

Signed sealed and delivered in presence of — John Bailey
James Bailey — William Bailey
James Bailey — Elizabeth Bailey (her mark)
John McClanahan
William Fleming
William Walker
John Deboo (his mark)

To Willoughby Newton, Richard Lee, and John Newton, Gent. Whereas John Bailey, William Bailey and Elizabeth Bailey the wife of John Bailey by their indenture of bargain and sale bearing even day with these presents have sold and conveyed unto Peter McClanahan the fee simple estate of a tract of land (except a burying place) lying in the County of Westmoreland containing 75 acres and whereas the said Elizabeth Bailey cannot conveniently travel to record to make acknowledgment. Witness, James Davenport, clerk of our said court the 22nd day of October.
Westmoreland Sct. We do hereby certify that in obedience to the writ hereto annexed we have examined Mrs. Elizabeth Bailey privily and apart from her husband and she doth acknowledge to us that the said conveyance is made on her part freely and voluntarily and she is willing the same be recorded. Given under our hands and seals the 27th day of October 1765.
Willoughby Newton
John Newton
At a court held for Westmoreland County the 30th day of June 1772 this indenture of feoffment and the memorandum of livery of seizen and receipt endorsed were proved by the oath of James Bailey a witness hereto and the same having been proved by two others witnesses in March 1766 are together with the commission annexed for taking the acknowledgment and privy examination of Elizabeth Bailey the wife of John Bailey party thereto and a certificate of execution thereof ordered to be recorded. Teste

Page 211.
Leasure Hall's Will
I Leasure Hall of the Parish of Cople and County of Westmoreland being sick and weak of body but of good and perfect sense and memory do make and ordain this to be my last will and testament.
Imprimis, I give to my daughter Ann Lewis five shillings sterling with what I have before given her.
Item I give to my daughter Mary Bailey five shillings sterling with what I have before given her.
Item I give unto my brother Ashton Hall, Negro man Ned for and during his natural life and after his death to my wife and if she dies without heir of my begetting, to my two daughters Ann and Mary.
Item I give unto my wife Joanna Lewis Hall, Negro girl Nan, and the use of all my estate be it real or personal for her natural life and after her death I give the use of it to my two daughters Ann and Mary for their lives and after their death to be equally divided between their lawful heirs.
I appoint my loving wife to be executrix of this my last will and testament. In witness whereof I have hereunto set my hand and seal this 27th day of January 1770.
Signed sealed and delivered in the presence of Leasure Hall
Samuel Rust, Robert Jeffries
Mary Beale (her mark), Samuel Mockridge (his mark)
At a court held for Westmoreland County the 30th day of June 1772 this will was proved according to law by the oaths of Samuel Rust and Robert Jeffries witnesses thereto and ordered to be recorded. Teste (NB executrix qualified in September 1773)

Page 212.
Wickliff & Wife to Thompson Indenture
This indenture made the 27th day of June 1772 between David Wickliff and Jane Wickliff his wife of the Parish of Washington in County of Westmoreland of the one part and William Thompson of the parish and county aforesaid of the other part. Witnessed that David Wickliff and Jane Wickliff his wife in consideration of 200 pounds current money has sold to William Thompson a tract or dividend of land lying part in Westmoreland and part in King George

Counties, containing 300 acres and bounded as followeth; beginning at a small cedar which stands by the stump of a red oak which was the reputed corner tree to this land according to a survey made by Edwin Conway, being part of a tract of land bought out of William Underwood's patent by Samuel Bromfield who was grandfather to Maximilian Robinson, extending thence West Southwest 160 poles, thence North 3° West 268 poles, thence East by North ¾° Northerly 320 poles, thence Southeast by South ½° Easterly 200 poles to the place it first began at. In witness whereof the said parties have hereunto set her hand and seals the day and year first above written.

Signed sealed and acknowledged in presence of / David Wickliff
John Etherington / Jane Wickliff (her mark)
William Nelson
Isaac Wickliff

At a court held for Westmoreland County the 30th day of June 1772 this indenture and receipt endorsed or acknowledged by David Wickliff and Jane Wickliff his wife parties thereto (she being first privily examined as the law directs) and ordered to be recorded. Teste

Page 214.

Alexander McGuire's Will

In the name of God, Amen, I Alexander McGuire of Cople Parish in County of Westmoreland being weak in body but of sound in mind and memory do make constitute appoint and ordain this my last will and testament in manner and form following.

Item I give unto my loving son Traverse McGuire all my cattle, young and old, to him and his heirs forever. Also, he should give his brother Alexander McGuire's son Robert McGuire one years schooling. Likewise, to give John McGuire's son William McGuire one years schooling. Likewise, Charles Scutt's son Thomas Foler Scutt one years schooling

I give and bequeath unto Traverse McGuire all my hogs, young and old.

Item I give unto my daughter Martha McGuire one small bed and furniture.

Item I give unto Traverse McGuire, two iron pots, together with all my sheep, young and old.

Item I leave my son Traverse McGuire my whole executor of this my last will and testament.

In witness whereof I have hereunto set my hand and seal this 27th of March 1772

Teste / Alexander McGuire (his mark)
Gerard Hutt
John Reynolds (his mark)
John Billings (his mark)

At a court held for Westmoreland County the 30th day of June 1772 this will was proved according to law by the oaths of Gerard Hutt and John Billings witnesses thereto and ordered to be recorded and on the motion of Traverse McGuire the executors therein named who made oath thereto according to law and together with the said Gerard Hutt his securities entered into and acknowledged bond with condition as the law directs, certificate is granted him for obtaining a probate thereof in due form. Teste

Page 215.

Courtney & Wife to Rust Indenture

This indenture made the 8th day of June 1772 between James Courtney and Margaret Courtney his wife of the County of Westmoreland and colony of Virginia of the one part and Peter Rust of the said county and colony of the other part. Witnesseth that James Courtney and Margaret Courtney his wife in consideration of 25 pounds current money of Virginia has sold to Peter Rust the tract of land and appurtenances thereunto belonging or the said James Courtney now lives lying in Yeocomico Neck and bounded by the land of Capt. Daniel Tebbs, George Rust, Peter Rust, and William Tebbs containing 100 acres. In witness whereof the said James Courtney and Margaret Courtney his wife have hereunto set their hands and seals the day and month and year first above written.

Signed sealed and delivered in the presence of / James Courtney

Samuel Rust, Thaddeus Jackson
Magdalene Rust, Mary Beale (her mark)
Memorandum, that James Courtney is to have his lifetime on that part of the above-mentioned land that's on the right hand of the road that leads into Yeocomico Neck and liberty of timber that's on the other side of the road for the use of the plantation, that is to say, hogshead timber, rails and firewood for his own use with[out] making any waste of it.
At a court held for Westmoreland County the 30th day of June 1772 this indenture and receipt endorsed or acknowledged by James Courtney partly thereto and ordered to be recorded. Teste

Page 217.
William Berkley's Will
The last will and testament of William Berkley age 45 years or thereabouts devise as followeth;
Item I give and bequeath unto my wife Peggy Berkley one full third of all my estate real and personal as her property forever.
Item I give and bequeath unto my son John Berkley the residue of my estate both real and personal as his property forever to be delivered him and his arrival at the age of 21 years but if he should die before he comes to of age then my wife should enjoy the whole.
It is my desire that my wife should possess my whole estate for the better maintenance of my son John Berkley until he be of age except my wife should marry and if so then is my will that my son should as soon as he thinks proper received to fool thirds of my estate as aforesaid.
I do constitute and appoint my wife Peggy Berkley and my son John Berkley executors of this my last will and testament. In witness thereof I have hereunto set my hand and seal the second day of November in the year of our Lord 1769.
William Nelson
John Nelson, Jr.
At a court held for Westmoreland County the 28th day July 1772 this will was proved according to law by the oaths of William Nelson and John Nelson, Jr., the witnesses thereto and ordered to be recorded and on the motion of Peggy Berkley and John Berkley the executors therein named who made oath thereto according to law he together with the said John Nelson, Jr., and William Nelson their securities entered into and acknowledged bond with condition as the law directs, certificate is granted them for obtaining a probate thereof in due form. Teste

Page 218.
Read to McKenney Lease
This indenture made the 28th day of July 1772 between Andrew Read of the Parish of Cople and County of Westmoreland, Planter of the one part and Vincent McKenney of the same parish and county, planter of the other part. Witnesseth that Andrew Read in consideration of five shillings and the rents and covenants herein after mentioned has demise and to farm let unto Vincent McKenney a tenement of land where Thomas Brown formerly lived containing by estimation 130 acres with all appurtenances thereunto belonging. To have and to hold the said premises from the day of the date hereof for and during the natural life of Vincent McKenney yielding and paying yearly the rent of 530 pounds of transfer tobacco at some convenient warehouse, the first payment to be made on the first day of January 1774; and a agrees to build a dwelling house and a corn house to be completed by Christmas next and to build for himself all other houses he may want on the said tenement and keep them in repair. In witness whereof the parties to these presents have interchangeably set their hand and fixed her seals the day month and year first above written. Signed sealed and delivered in the presence of us Andrew Read
Vincent McKenney (his mark)
At a court held for Westmoreland County the 28th day of July 1772 this indenture of lease

was acknowledged by Andrew Read and Vincent McKenney the parties thereto and ordered to be recorded.
Test James Davenport CWC

Page 219.
John Collingsworth's Will
In the name of God, Amen, I John Collinsworth, Sr., of the County of Westmoreland and Parish of Cople, planter being weak in body but of perfect mind and memory do make and ordain this my last will and testament.
Item all the land I hold between the division line that divides me and Nathaniel Butler and my nephew John Collinsworth and my nephew Thomas Collinsworth, to the head of the creek where the marsh forks, thence running up the marsh to the spring from thence to the road by the same branch, from thence running up the east fork of the said branch to the line that divides me and John Brinnon and the land that belongs to me after my brother Willoughby Collinsworth's death, I give to my son Thomas Collinsworth.
Item all the land I hold between the spring branch and the corner that hath been mentioned to the line that divides me and John Washington and John Brinnon I leave to my son John Collinsworth.
If my son Thomas Collinsworth dies without heir his part of the land I leave to my son Willoughby Collinsworth.
If my son John Collinsworth dies without heir his part of the land I leave to my son Jesse Collinsworth.
If they all four shall die without lawful heir then the above land I leave to my son Vincent Collinsworth.
If all my son shall die without lawful heir then the above land I leave to my three daughters, Sarah Collinsworth, Peggy Collinsworth, and Martha Collinsworth.
All my movable estate I leave to my wife Margaret Collinsworth in my children to be equally divided amongst them.
Willoughby Collinsworth John Collinsworth
James Clark
John Brinnon
Lastly to conclude I nominate and appoint my wife Margaret Collinsworth and son Thomas Collinsworth soul executors of this my last will and testament. My desire is that my son Thomas Collinsworth should give my four youngest children one years schooling a piece, to take care of his mother as long as she lives and all the children until they come of age and to live together.
In witness whereof I have hereunto set my hand and seal this ninth day of October 1766
Signed sealed and delivered in presence of John Collinsworth
Willoughby Collinsworth
James Clark
John Brinnon
At a court held for Westmoreland County the 28th day of July 1772 this will was proved according to law by the oaths of Willoughby Collinsworth and John Brinnon witnesses thereto and ordered to be recorded and on the motion of Thomas Collinsworth one of the executors therein named who made oath thereto according to law and together with John Brinnon, Jr., and Andrew Read his securities entered into and acknowledged bond with condition as the law directs, certificate is granted him for obtaining a probate thereof in due form. Teste

Page 221.
Kendrick to Kendrick Deed of Gift
I William Jarvis Kendrick of the Parish of Cople in County of Westmoreland for the natural love and affection which I have and do bear towards my loving daughter Elizabeth Kendrick

of the parish and county aforesaid do give by these presents all my right and interest to the sundry goods and chattels hereafter mentioned; my crop of corn and tobacco now growing, one horse, one feather bed and furniture, one half dozen plates, two dishes, two basons , four chairs, two chests, one oval table, three pots, one frying pan, a box iron, 10 head of hogs, one half dozen geese, two piggins, and one pail. In witness whereof I have hereunto set my hand and seal this 27th day of July 1772.
Signed sealed and delivered in presence of William Jarvis Kendrick
Daniel Tebbs
Samuel Rust
Daniel Bennett
At a court held for Westmoreland County the 28th day of July 1772 this deed of gift was proved by the oaths of Samuel Rust and Daniel Bennett witnesses thereto and ordered to be recorded. Teste

Page 222.
Rust to Rust Deed of Gift
Whereas Charnock Cox of the County of Westmoreland, deceased out of the natural love and affection by his last will and testament did bequeath unto his granddaughter and my daughter Molly Rust, since deceased, being young and intestate, Negro woman Sarah with her future increase, and I supposing that upon her death the said Negro woman and her increase did lawfully descend unto my other children in equal proportions did value the said Negro and her issue and paid unto my son Peter Rust the sum of 18 pounds current money as his proportional part, but since having advised by sundry persons skilled in the law I am informed that the writ of inheritance by law is invested in my son Peter having been my eldest son and heir at law to his sister exclusive of all others. I do hereby upon his repaying the above said sum of 18 pounds warrant and defend assign unto my said son Peter Rust his heirs and assigns the said Negro Sarah together with her five children; Jenny, Settles, Nell, Benn and Natt, together with all their future increase. In witness whereof I have hereunto set my hand and seal the 29th day of July 1772. Samuel Rust
At a court continued and held for Westmoreland County the 29th day of July 1772 this deed was acknowledged by Samuel Rust party thereto and ordered to be recorded. Test

Page 223.
Quisenbury to Pope Deed of Gift
I Humphrey Quisenbury of the Parish of Washington in County of Westmoreland, planter in consideration of the true love and paternal affection which I bear unto my beloved daughter Jane Pope wife of Lawrence Pope of the Parish of Lunenburg in County of Richmond as well as other viable considerations me hereunto especially moving have given by these presents by six Negro slaves; Negro lads Harry and Charles, Negro woman Lucy and her three children; James, Kate and Hannah. In witness whereof I the said Humphrey Quisenbury have hereunto set my hand and seal this 10th day of August 1772.
Signed sealed and delivered in presence of Humphrey Quisenbury
John Perkins
John Omohundro
George Tiffey
At a court held for Westmoreland County the 25th day of August 1772 this deed of gift was acknowledged by Humphrey Quisenbury party thereto and ordered to be recorded.
Test James Davenport Cl Cur

Page 224.
John Harrison's Will
In the name of God, Amen, I John Harrison of the County of Westmoreland being sick of body but of sound and perfect memory do make this my last will and testament in manner

and form following this fourth day of April 1769.
Imprimis, I give and bequeath to the heirs of my son George Harrison one shilling sterling is therefore part of my estate not yet received.
Item I give all my lands to my son John Harrison and the heirs of his body forever; and for want of such heirs my will is that my daughter Abigail Harrison shall have the above said lands vested in her and her heirs; and in case they both should depart this life without heirs that the land should descend to my son Robert Harrison and his heirs.
Further my will is that my daughter Abigail Harrison shall and may live on my land with my son John Harrison or on any part of my land as long as she live single and if he is willing that she may live in the house with him then she is to have no more the land that is useful to support her.
Item I give to my son John Harrison two feather beds and furniture, and a large cherry tree table.
Item I give to my daughter Abigail Harrison the bed and furniture I commonly lie on, a cupboard, and a young cow and calf.
Item I give to my grandson Robin? Harper one years schooling provided his father or any other friend will accommodate him for the year while at school.
Item I give the residue of my estate after my lawful debts and legacies are paid to be equally divided between all my children and their lawful appears, the heirs of my son George Harrison excepted, and I do make and ordain my son John Harrison, my whole sole and entire executor of this my last will and testament made by me.
Signed sealed and acknowledged in presence of John Harrison
Richard Lee, Reuben Jordan
Richard Jackson, Joseph Lane
At a court held for Westmoreland County the 25th day of August 1772 this will was proved according to law by the oaths of Richard Lee and Reuben Jordan witnesses thereto and ordered to be recorded and on the motion of John Harrison the executor therein named who made oath thereto according to law and together with Samuel Walker his security entered into and acknowledged bond with condition as the law directs, certificate is granted him for obtaining a probate thereof in due form. Test

Page 225.
Corbin to Hamilton Indenture
This Indenture made the 22nd day of November 1771 between Hannah Corbin of Cople Parish and County of Westmoreland, Gentlewoman of the one part and Hugh Hamilton of the same parish and county, Gent., of the other part. Witnesseth that Hannah Corbin in consideration of the rents and covenants herein mentioned has demised and to farm let unto Hugh Hamilton a tenement of land now in his possession containing 40 acres. To have and to hold the said land, yielding and paying yearly and every year during his natural life, paying the rent of 20 pounds current money [payment date not mentioned]. In witness whereof the parties have hereunto interchangeably set their hands and affixed their seals the day month and year first above written.
Signed sealed and delivered in the presence of Hannah Corbin
Richard Lee Hugh Hamilton
Reuben Jordan
John Berryman
At a court held for Westmoreland County the 25th day of August 1772 this indenture of lease was proved by the oath of John Berryman a witness thereto and the same having been before proved by the oath [xxx] Witnesses and ordered to be recorded. Teste

Page 229.
Garner to Morgan Mortgage
I James Garner, son of Thomas Garner and the County of Westmoreland in consideration of

242 pounds 2 shillings and 9 pence current money of Virginia has sold unto Daniel Morgan; Negro woman Beck, and her two sons James and Daniel, Negro boy Anthony, Negro child Sam, 3 cows , 2 drought steers, 3 yearlings marked with a crop and over keel, one gray horse, 3 mares (two white and one black), 16 hogs marked as above, 3 feather beds and furniture, as also all my furniture of every kind whatsoever. In witness whereof I have hereunto set my hand and seal this 25th day of August 1772.
Signed sealed and delivered in presence of James Garner
Benjamin Branham
George Rust
Provided always and upon the condition that if the aforesaid James Garner shall well and truly pay to the said Daniel Morgan the sum of 108, 18 shillings and 6 pence ½ penny with the lawful interest for the same at the rate of 5% p/annum from 24th day of July last past on or before the 25th day of December next ensuing after the date of the aforesaid indenture then the said indenture and everything therein contained shall cease and be void. In witness whereof the parties aforesaid have hereunto set their hands and seals the day and year first above written.
James Garner
Daniel Morgan
At a court held for Westmoreland County the 25th day of August 1772 this deed was acknowledged by James Garner and Daniel Morgan parties thereto and ordered to be recorded. Teste James Davenport Cl Cur

Page 230.
Brown & Wife to Hutt Indenture
This indenture made the 26th day of September 1772 between William Brown and Margaret Brown his wife of the Parish of Cople and County of Westmoreland, planter of the one part and John Hutt of the aforesaid parish and county of the other part. Witnesseth that William Brown and Margaret Brown his wife in consideration of 240 pounds current money has sold to John Hutt a tract of land containing 200 acres and lying in the Parish of Cople and County of Westmoreland, being the plantation that William Fryer bought of Jacob Sutton, adjoining to the land of John Hutt. In witness whereof the said parties first above mentioned to these presents have interchangeably set their hands and seals the day and year above written.
Signed sealed and delivered in the presence of us William Brown
Thomas Edwards Margaret Brown (her mark)
John Smith
At a court held for Westmoreland County the 29th day of September 1772, this indenture of feoffment and memorandum of livery of seizen were acknowledged by William Brown and Margaret Brown his wife parties thereto (she being privy examined as the law directs) and ordered to be recorded. Teste

Page 232.
Brown to Hutt Indenture
This indenture made the 26th day of September 1772 between William Brown, executor of John Brown, deceased, pursuant to the last will and testament of the Parish of Cople and County of Westmoreland, planter of the one part and John Hutt of the aforesaid parish and county aforesaid. Witnesseth that William Brown, executor in consideration of 64 pounds 15 shillings current money has sold to John Hutt all that plantation and tract of land containing 50 acres lying in the Parish of Cople and County of Westmoreland being the plantation of Thomas Blundell's now the property of John Brown, deceased and adjoining to the land of John Hutt and Andrew Read.
In witness whereof the said parties first above mentioned to these presents have interchangeably set their hands and seals the day and year above written.
Signed sealed and delivered in the presence of us William Brown

Thomas Edwards
George McKenney
John Smith
At a court held for Westmoreland County the 29th day of September 1772, this indenture of feoffment and memorandum of livery of seizen were acknowledged by William Brown party thereto and ordered to be recorded. Teste

Page 235.
Lamkin to Wife & Children Deed of Gift
I Matthew Lamkin of the county of Washington and Parish of Cople and for the natural love and affection which I bear to my wife and four sons and for many other causes, me especially moving doe make the following gifts;
To my wife Frances Lamkin, 170 acres of land, 100 acres whereof my father purchased of George Cox and Ellen Cox his wife, the other 70 acres which fell to me by my mother Ann Lamkin, during her life and after her death I give the 170 acres to my three sons, George Lamkin, Charles Lamkin, and Matthew Lamkin in equal proportions.
I also give to my wife Frances Lamkin, Negro woman Frank during her life and after her death to my son Matthew Lamkin with her future increase.
I give to my son Benedict Lamkin, Negroes; Old Ealse, Ned and Hannah with her increase.
I give to my son George Lamkin, Negroes, Sam and Jude and her increase.
I give to my son Charles Lamkin, three Negroes; Cooper, Will and Young Ealse and her increase
I give to my son Matthew Lamkin, Negro boy Ben and Negro girl Sue with her increase.
I give to my loving wife Frances Lamkin for the causes aforesaid, my household furniture with my stock of every kind to her own use but if either of my sons which I have by my now present wife should die before they arrive to the age prescribed by law to make any legal devise, that then the surviving children which I have with my present wife Frances Lamkin to have an equal division of such estate as aforesaid given. In witness whereof I have hereunto set my hand and seal this 28th September 1772.
In the presence of Matthew Lamkin
Hugh Hamilton
Fleet Cox
John Middleton
John Hobson Fallin
At a court held for Westmoreland County the 29th day of September 1772 this deed of gift was proved by the oaths of Hugh Hamilton, Fleet Cox and John Hobson Fallin witnesses thereto and ordered to be recorded. Teste

Page 236.
John Muse's Will
I John Muse the County of Westmoreland Parish of Washington, planter do ordain constitute and appoint this to be my last will and testament.
Imprimis, I give unto my son Nicholas Muse the tract of land whereon I now live to him and his heirs and for want of such heirs then to my son James Muse.
Desire that my daughter Mary Muse may have the use benefit and advantage of a tract of land that John Nelson now rents on the head of Mattox during her life.
Item I give and bequeath unto my two sons James Muse and Thomas Muse all my land lying on the head of Mattox to be equally divided between them.
Item I give and bequeath unto my son John Muse and his heirs the tract of land formerly Humphrey Pope's lying near Mattox Church and for want of such heirs then to my son Nicholas Muse.
Item I give and bequeath unto my son Nicholas Muse [Negro] Fill and Suck.

Item I give and bequeath unto my son James Muse, Negroes; James, Sarah and Sharpess.
Item I give and bequeath unto my daughter Mary Muse, Negroes; Jacob, George and Mildred.
Item I give and bequeath unto my son John Muse, Negroes; Ben, Lett, Davy and Charles.
Item I give and bequeath unto my son Thomas Muse, Negroes; Daniel, Ealse, Patt and Little Fill.
Item I give and bequeath to my son Nicholas Muse my still.
Item I give and bequeath unto my daughter Mary Muse, my riding chair, sorrel and gray horse.
Item I give and bequeath unto my son John Muse my black horse.
Item I give and bequeath unto my son James Muse by maple desk.
My desire is that all the remainder of my movable estate may be kept together while such time my debts are paid off and there to be equally divided between my five children and not appraised.
Lastly, I appoint my two sons Nicholas Muse and James Muse, executors of this my last will and testament. In witness whereof I have hereunto set my hand and seal this fifth day of January 1772.
In presence of John Muse
Benjamin Weeks, Charles Weeks
Thomas King, Nicholas Muse
At a court held for Westmoreland County the 29th day of December 1772 this will was proved according to the law by the oath of Thomas King and Nicholas Muse witness thereto and ordered to be recorded and on the motion of Nicholas Muse one of the executors therein named who made oath thereto according to law and together with Thomas Chilton and Joseph Price his securities entered into and acknowledged bond with condition as the law directs, certificate is granted him for obtaining a probate thereof in due form. Teste.

Page 238.
Sorrell & Wife to Turberville Indenture
This indenture made the 24th day December 1772 between Thomas Sorrell and Mildred Sorrell his wife of Parish of Cople and County of Westmoreland of the one part and John Turberville of the aforesaid county and parish of the other part. Witnesseth that Thomas Sorrell and Mildred Sorrell his wife in consideration of 200 pounds current money of Virginia sold to John Turberville the tract of land lying in the aforesaid County of Westmoreland and Parish of Cople containing 186 acres (the family graveyard with the way to and from the same excepted) and bounded as follows; on the south side of Nominy mill pond, on the north side of John Augustine Washington's mill pond, and the land purchased by the late Mr. John Bushrod of John Sorrell, deceased on the east, and west by the lands of the said John Turberville, which said land fell to the said Thomas Sorrell by inheritance from his father John Sorrell, late of the County of Westmoreland, dying intestate.
Signed sealed and delivered in presence of Thomas Sorrell
John of Augustine Washington Mildred Sorrell
Joseph Lane
Lancelot Lee
George Glascock, Jr.
William Habron
John Pope, Jr.
To Richard Lee, John Augustine Washington and Joseph Lane, Gent. Whereas Thomas Sorrell and Mildred Sorrell his wife by their indenture of bargain and sale have sold and conveyed unto John Turberville, Gent., The fee simple estate of 186 acres lying in the Parish of Cople and County of Westmoreland and whereas the said Mildred cannot conveniently travel to record to make acknowledgment. Therefore, we do give unto you or any two or more of you power to receive the acknowledgment which the said Mildred Sorrell shall be willing to

make. Witness James Davenport, clerk of our said court this 24th day of December 1772. Westmoreland County, to wit; by virtue of a commission to was directed from the court of Westmoreland bearing date the 24th day of December 1772 and hereunto annexed, we did personally go to Mildred Sorrell wife of Thomas Sorrell and did examine her separate and apart from her husband touching her relinquishment of her right of dower in and to the lands and tenements conveyed by the deed and she declared that she did the same freely and voluntarily without persuasion or threats and she is willing that the said deed of should be recorded in the said County Court of Westmorland. Certified under our hands and seals this 24th day of December 1772
John Augustine Washington
Joseph Lane
At a court held for Westmoreland County the 29th day of December 1772 this indenture and receipt endorsed were acknowledged by Thomas Sorrell party thereto and together with the commission the next for taking the acknowledgment and privy examination of Mildred Sorrell the wife of Thomas Sorrell and a certificate of the execution thereof ordered to be recorded.
Test James Davenport CWC

Page 241.
Brown & Edwards Bond for Division of Land
We William Brown and Thomas Edwards of Cople Parish and Westmoreland County am held and firmly bound unto Thomas Templeman of the parish and county aforesaid in the full and just sum of 1000 pounds current money of Virginia to be paid to him his heirs and assigns to which payment well and truly to be made, we bind ourselves. In witness whereof we have hereunto set our hands and seals this sixth day of August 1772. Now the above obligation is such that if the above bounden William Brown shall well and truly stand to and abide by the division in the lands that now lie in dispute between him and William Brown and Thomas Templeman, which division was mutually agreed on by the said Brown and the said Templeman. Now the said Brown is to have and to hold all the remainder part and parcel of the land that now lie in dispute, excepting that parcel or tract that William Fryer bought of Jacob Remy that the said Thomas Templeman agrees to take for his part and the said William Brown his heirs and assigns to have and hold all the remainder tracts or parcels of the said lands with all profits thereto belonging and to be fully satisfied with the same then the above obligation to be void and of non-effect or otherwise to remain in full force and virtue in law.
Signed sealed and delivered in presence of William Brown
Gerard Hutt Thomas Edwards
George Cavender
George McKenney
At a court held for Westmoreland County the 29th day of December 1772 this bond was proved by the oath of Gerard Hutt and George McKenney witnesses thereto and ordered to be recorded. Teste

County, Virginia Deeds & Wills 1768-1773; DB-15 {Abstract by Mike Marshall}; Page 241.
Templeman & Brown Bond for Division of Land
We Thomas Templeman and John Hutt of Cople Parish and Westmoreland County am held and firmly bound unto William Brown of the parish and county aforesaid in the fall and just some of 1000 pounds current money of Virginia to be paid to him to which payment well and truly to be made we bind ourselves. In witness whereof we have hereunto set our hands and seals this sixth day of August 1772.
Now the above obligation is such that if the above bound Thomas Templeman shall well and truly stand and abide by the division in the lands that now lie in dispute between him and the said Thomas Templeman and the said William Brown which division was mutually agreed on by the said Templeman and the said Brown, now the said Thomas Templeman is to have and

to hold all that parcel or tract of land he now lives on which William Fryer bought of Jacob Remy as his full part with all profits thereto belonging without having any right or claim to any other part of the said land that now lie in dispute, and that he the said Templeman shall at all times be fully satisfied with same then the above obligation to be void and of non-effect otherwise to remain in full force and virtue in law.

Signed sealed and delivered in the presence of us Thomas Templeman
Gerard Hutt
George Cavender
George McKenney

At a court held for Westmoreland County the 29th day of December 1772 this bond was proved by the oath of Gerard Hutt and George McKenney witnesses thereto and ordered to be recorded. Teste

Page 243.

Stoner & Wife to Spark Indenture

This indenture made the 19th day of November 1772 between Peter Stoner of the County of Cumberland and Frances Stoner his wife of the one part and Alexander Spark of the County of Westmoreland the other part. Witnesseth that Peter Stoner and Frances Stoner his wife in consideration of 550 pounds current money of Virginia have sold and released to Alexander Spark all that tract situated in the County of Westmoreland and Parish of Cople whereof the Courthouse of the said County is part. Beginning at a small branch which divides this land from the land now the property of Capt. John Gordon, thence down the meanders of the said branch to the main run of Solomon Redman's Mill Pond, thence down the said main run to the mouth of another branch which divides this land from the land of Richard Neale formerly of Sturman, thence up the said branch to a marked tree standing at the head of it, thence South 36° East 38 ¼ poles, thence South 22 ½° West 44 poles, thence 16 ½° East 22 poles to the head of a branch which divides this land from the land of George Mitchell, thence down the said branch to a small gum, a corner tree to this land, the land of George Mitchell, John Jordan and Solomon Redman, thence South 35° East 96 poles to Dr. Flood's mill run, now in the possession of George Turberville, thence up the said mill run to a branch which divides this land from the land of Joel Sanford, thence up the said branch to a gum tree corner to this land, Joel Sanford's and the land of Mr. Edward Ransdell, thence along Mr. Ransdell's line to a chestnut standing on the road leading to John Sanford's, thence crossing the said road North 49° West 132 poles to a chestnut near John Sanford's fence, and thence to the beginning place, containing 584 acres. In witness whereof the parties to these presents have hereunto set their hands and seals the day and year first above written.

Sealed and delivered in presence of us Peter Stoner
John Turberville Frances Stoner
Joseph Lane
William Keene
George Jackson (his mark)
Mary Lane

To Richard Lee, John Turberville and Joseph Lane of the Westmoreland, Gent. Whereas Peter Stoner and Frances Stoner his wife by their indenture of bargain and sale dated the 19th day of November 1772 have sold and conveyed unto Alexander Spark the fee simple estate of 584 acres being in the Parish of Cople and County of Westmoreland and whereas the said Frances cannot conveniently travel to our court to make acknowledgment. Therefore, we do give unto you or any two of you power to receive the acknowledgment which the said Frances Stoner shall be willing to make before you of the conveyance. Witnesseth James Davenport, clerk of our said court the 20th day of November 1772.

Westmoreland County Sct. By virtue of the above writ to us directed we did personally go to Frances Stoner and before us she did acknowledge this indenture hereunto annexed to be her act and deed and that she did the same freely and voluntarily without the persuasion or

threats of her husband and was willing that the same should be recorded in the County Court of Westmoreland. Although which we do hereby certified under our hands and seals this 20th day of November 1772.
John Turberville
Joseph Lane
At a court held for Westmoreland County the 29th day of December 1772 this indenture and receipt endorsed proved by the oath of George Jackson a witness thereto and the same having been before proved by the oaths of two other of the witnesses thereto are together with the commission annexed for taking the acknowledgment and privy examination of Frances Stoner the wife of Peter Stoner party thereto and a certificate of the execution thereof ordered to be recorded. Teste

Page 247.
Rust & Wife to Spark Indenture
This indenture made the 19th day of November 1772 between Jeremiah Rust and Frances Rust his wife of the one part and Alexander Spark of the said County of the other part. Witnesseth that Jeremiah Rust and Frances Rust his wife in consideration of five shillings have sold and released unto Alexander Spark all the right and title of dower which the said Frances Rust hath to all the land belonging which William Stewart Minor; the late husband of the said Frances did possess lying in the Parish of Cople and County of Westmoreland which the Courthouse of the said County is part, which land is more described in a deed made and granted by Peter Stoner and his wife Frances for the said Alexander Spark bearing date with these presents. In witness whereof the parties to these presents have hereunto set their hands and seals the day and year first above written.
Sealed and delivered in the presence of us — Jeremiah Rust
Joseph Lane — Frances Rust
Mary Lane
William Keene
George Jackson (his mark)
To Richard Lee, John Turberville and Joseph Lane of the County of Westmoreland, Gent. Whereas Jeremiah Rust and Frances Rust his wife by their indenture of bargain and sale bearing date the 19th day of November 1772 have sold and conveyed unto Alexander Spark the fee simple estate of 194 acres of land in the Parish of Cople and County of Westmoreland being one third part (the same being her dower) of all that tract of land which Peter Stoner has sold and conveyed unto the said Alexander Spark containing 584 acres and whereas Frances Rust cannot conveniently travel to our court to make acknowledgment. Therefore, we do give unto you or any two or more of you power to receive the acknowledgment which the said Frances Rust shall be willing to make. Witness James Davenport, clerk of our said court the 20th day of November 1772.
Westmoreland County Sct; by virtue of the above writ to us directed we did personally go to Frances Rust and before us she did acknowledge the indenture hereunto annexed to be her act and deed and that she did the same freely and voluntarily without the persuasion or threats of her husband in the same should be recorded in the County Court of Westmoreland. Although which we hereby certify under our hands and seals this 20th day of November 1772.
John Turberville
Joseph Lane
At a court held for Westmoreland County the 29th day of December 1772 this indenture and receipt endorsed or proved by oath of George Jackson a witness thereto and the same having been before proved by two other witnesses are together with the commission annexed for taking the acknowledgment and privy examination of Frances Rust the wife of Jeremiah Rust party thereto and a certificate of the execution thereof ordered to be recorded. Test

Page 249.
John Hutt's Will
In the name of God, Amen, I John Hutt of Cople Parish and the County of Westmoreland being weak in body but of sound mind and memory do make constitute and appoint and ordain this my last will and testament in manner and form following.
Item I give and bequeath to my son John Hutt and my son Gerard Robinson Hutt all the land I bought of Gerard Davis, likewise the land I bought of William Brown, and likewise the land I bought of the executor of John Brown, deceased, estate, to be equally divided between their heirs.
Item I give and bequeath unto my son William Hutt, John Hutt and Gerard Robinson Hutt, and my daughter Elizabeth Robinson Hutt, all the remainder of my estate which consists of Negroes, stock of all kinds, still, household furniture, ready cash, debts due, unto them and their heirs lawfully begotten.
Item it is my desire that Thomas Edwards, my son William Hutt, and my brother Gerard Hutt executors of this my last will and testament. In witness whereof I have hereunto set my hand and seal this third day of December 1772
John Crabb, Sr. John Hutt
George McKenney
John Smith
At a court held for Westmoreland County the 29th day December 1772 this will was proved according to law by the oaths of George McKenney and John Smith witnesses thereto and ordered to be recorded and on the motion of Thomas Edwards and Gerard Hutt two of the executors therein named who made oath thereto according to law and together with John Turberville and Solomon Redman their securities entered into and acknowledged by with condition as the law directs, certificate is granted them for obtaining a probate thereof in due form. Teste

Page 250.
Minor to Redman Indenture
This indenture made the 29th day of December 1772 between William Minor of the Parish of Lunenburg in the County of Richmond, planter of the one part and Solomon Redman of the Parish of Cople and the County of Westmoreland, millwright of the other part. Witnesseth that William Minor in consideration of 55 pounds Virginia currency has sold to Solomon Redman all that tract of land in the Parish of Cople and County of Westmoreland consisting of 75 acres. In witness whereof the parties to these presents have interchangeably set their hands and seals the day and year first above written.
Signed sealed and delivered in the presence of us William Minor
Richard Neale Solomon Redman
Henry Sisson Redman
John Perkins
At a court held for Westmoreland County the 26th day of January 1773 this indenture was proved by the oath of Richard Neale, Henry Sisson Redman and John Perkins the witnesses thereto and ordered to be recorded. Teste

Page 251.
Rust & Wife to Fauntleroy Indenture
This indenture made the 2nd day of December 1772 between Jeremiah Rust and Frances Rust his wife of the Parish of Cople and County of Westmoreland of the one part and William Fauntleroy, Sr., of the Parish of Lunenburg and County of Richmond of the other part. Witnesseth that Jeremiah Rust and Frances Rust his wife in consideration of 200 pounds current money of Virginia has sold unto William Fauntleroy, Sr., all that tract lying in the Parish of Cople and County of Westmoreland containing by estimation 75 acres being the

same formerly belonging to Daniel McCarty, Esq. and by him sold to the said Jeremiah Rust; the said land lying on Yeocomico River and joining to the lands of Jeremiah Garland Bailey and the lands of Peter Mullins together with all appurtenances. In witness whereof the said Jeremiah Rust and Frances Rust his wife party to these presents have hereunto set their hands and seals the day and year above written.
Signed sealed and delivered in presence of Jeremiah Rust
Griffin Fauntleroy, Peter Stoner
Griffin Fauntleroy, John Crabb
Richard Lee, Reuben Jordan
Joseph Lane, Richard Lingan Hall
To Richard Lee, John Augustine Washington and Joseph Lane, Gent. Whereas Jeremiah Rust of the County of Westmoreland and Frances Rust his wife by their indenture of feoffment bearing date the second day of December 1772 have sold and conveyed unto William Fauntleroy of the County of Richmond, Gent., The fee simple estate of 75 acres of land with the appurtenances lying in the Parish of Cople and County of Westmoreland and whereas the said Frances Rust cannot conveniently travel to our court to make acknowledgment. Therefore, we do give unto you or any two or more of you power to receive the acknowledgment which the said Frances Rust shall be willing to make before you. Witness, James Davenport, clerk of our said court the third day December.
Westmoreland County Sct. By virtue of the above writ to us directed we did personally go to Frances Rust wife of Jeremiah Rust and did examine her separate and apart from her husband and she acknowledged the indenture hereunto annexed to be her act and deed and that she did the same freely and voluntarily without the persuasion or threat of her husband and was willing that the same should be recorded in the County Court of Westmoreland. We do hereby certify under our hands and seals this 12th day of December 1772.
Richard Lee
Joseph Lane
At a court held for Westmoreland County the 26th day of January 1773 this indenture in the memorandum of livery of seizen endorsed were proved by the oaths of Griffin Fauntleroy, Joseph Lane and Richard Lee witnesses thereto and together with a commission annexed for taking the acknowledgment and privy examination of Frances Rust the wife of the within named Jeremiah Rust and a certificate of the execution thereof ordered to be recorded. Teste

Page 255.
<u>Lamkin to Lamkin Deed of Gift</u>
I Ashton Lamkin of Westmoreland County for diverse good causes and valuable considerations I do grant and confirm unto my sister Jeane Lamkin, Negro girl Winney but in case my sister should die without lawful heir that the said Negro should fall and descend to my sister Molly Lamkin and in case she dies without lawful heirs then the Negroe should fall and descend to Tilda Stott daughter to Tabitha Stott. In witness whereof I have hereunto set my hand and seal this 26th day of January 1773.
Signed sealed and delivered in the presence of us Ashton Lamkin
Solomon Redman
William Harrison
Daniel Bennett
Mary Barnett
At a court held for Westmoreland County the 26th day of January 1773 this deed of gift was proved by the oath of Solomon Redman, William Harrison and Mary Barnett witnesses thereto and ordered to be recorded. Teste

Page 256.
<u>Lamkin to Lamkin Deed of Gift</u>

I Ashton Lamkin of Westmoreland County for diverse good causes and valuable considerations I do grant and confirm unto my sister Molly Lamkin, Negro girl Doll but in case my sister should die without lawful heir that the said Negro should fall and descend to my sister Jeane Lamkin and in case she dies without lawful heirs then the Negroe should fall and descend to Tilda Stott daughter to Tabitha Stott. In witness whereof I have hereunto set my hand and seal this 26th day of January 1773.

Signed sealed and delivered in the presence of us Ashton Lamkin
Solomon Redman
William Harrison
Daniel Bennett

At a court held for Westmoreland County the 26th day of January 1773 this deed of gift was proved by the oath of Solomon Redman, William Harrison and Daniel Bennett witnesses thereto and ordered to be recorded. Teste

Page 256.

Asbury to McGinnis Indenture of Apprenticeship

this indenture made the 26th day of January 1773 between Thomas Asbury of the County of Richmond of the one part and Richard Schooler McGinnis of the said county, wheelwright of the other part. Witnessed that Thomas Asbury has bound himself an apprentice unto Richard Schooler McGinnis until he arrives at the age of 21 years who agrees to teach the said Thomas Asbury the business of a wheelwright. In witness whereof the parties to these presents have interchangeably set their hands and seals the day and year first above written.

Sealed and delivered in presence of us Thomas Asbury
R. Parker Richard Schooler McGinnis

At a court held for Westmoreland County the 26th day of January 1773 this indenture of apprenticeship was acknowledged by Thomas Asbury and Richard Schooler McGinnis parties thereto and ordered to be recorded. Test

Page 257.

White & Son to White Indenture

This indenture made the 18th day of March 1772 between Mary White, widow and relict of Daniel White late of the County of King George, who dying intestate and George White, son and heir at law of the said Daniel of the one part and Lovell White of the County of Westmoreland of the other part. Witnesseth that Mary White in consideration of 5 pounds and the said George White in consideration of 55 pounds have sold unto Lovell White all that tract of land in the County of Westmoreland which the said Daniel White died seized and possessed, containing 190 acres and bounded as follows; beginning upon Attopin Dam, in the line between Daniel White the elder and Thomas Pratt, thence along a lane over to the Black Swamp, thence up the swamp to the dividing line between the said Daniel White and William Marders, thence along the said line to Berryman's Dam and from thence to the beginning, including the whole tract of land of which the said Daniel White died possessed of together with all and appurtenances. In witness whereof the said Mary White and George White have hereunto set their hands and seals the day and year above written.

Signed sealed and acknowledge in presents of George White
James Brown Mary White (her mark)
Benjamin Thomas, James Dodd (his mark)

At a court held for Westmoreland County the 30th day of March 1773 this indenture and the receipt endorsed were proved by the oath of Benjamin Thomas a witness thereto and the same having been before proved by the two other witnesses and ordered to be recorded. Teste

Page 258.

John Nash's Will

In the name of God, Amen, I John Nash being very sick and weak but of perfect sense and memory do make and ordain this my last will and testament.

Item I give to Solomon Billings my cunnue [canoe]

Item I give all the rest of my estate to my beloved wife Ann Nash to dispose of as she thinks proper.

I leave my beloved wife Ann Nash and my friend Moore Bragg my executors of this my last will and testament February 24, 1773

Thomas Edwards, Jeremiah Nash John Nash (his mark)

Ann Nash (her mark)

At a court held for Westmoreland County the 30th day of March 1773 this will was proved according to law by the oaths of Jeremiah Nash and Ann Nash witnesses thereto and ordered to be recorded and on the motion of Ann Nash and Moore Bragg the executors therein named who made oath thereto according to law and together with Nathaniel Nash and William Griggs their securities entered into and acknowledged bond with condition as the law directs, certificate is granted them for obtaining a probate thereof in due form. Teste

Page 259.

George Lamkin's Nuncupative Will

On the 22nd day of December 1772 George Lamkin being sick but in perfect sense desired of his wife Agnes Lamkin, Thomas Matheny and Youell Gilbert, these being present to have his estate disposed of in the following manner provided he should not have an opportunity of leaving his will made which he had not for that night he was taken out of his senses and continued so till he departed this life, but desired his estate given in the following manner.

He gave to his wife Agnes Lamkin her widowhood all his estate giving his children a maintenance out of it and if she should marry to have but a child's part and the remaining part of the estate to be equally divided between his daughter Lucy Lamkin and his son Youell Lamkin;

and his trusty friends Thomas Matheny and Youell Gilbert to be his executors.

Agnes Lamkin Thomas Metheny
Youell Gilbert

At a court held for Westmoreland County the 30th day of March 1773 this writing purporting the nuncupative will of George Lamkin, deceased was proved according to law by the oaths of Thomas Matheny and Youell Gilbert witnesses thereto and the executors named in the said will (they having previously refused to take upon themselves the burthen of the execution thereof) in order to be recorded, and on the motion of Agnes Lamkin, the widow and relict of the testator who made oath thereto according to law and together with John Bailey and Thomas Matheny her securities entered into and acknowledged bond with condition as the law directs, certificate is granted for obtaining letters of administration of the estate of the said testator with of said will annexed in due form. Teste

Page 265.

Dolman to Dolman Deed of Gift

I William Dolman of the County of Westmoreland and Parish of Cople for diverse good causes me hereunto moving and more especially for the natural love and affection which I have and do bear unto my mother Sarah Dolman of the Parish and County aforesaid do freely and truly give to her all my whole right title and property which I have or do claim to all the freehold and leasehold estate which was given by my uncle John Henry Dolman, late of the Parish of St. Luke in the County of Middlesex, in Great Britain, in his last will and testament to my father Thomas Dolman, late of the County of Westmoreland, deceased; for and during her natural life or the time that she shall remain widow but in case she should marry again in the said estate is to return to me. After my mother's decease or her widowhood to give and allow my brother Thomas Sturman Dolman his heirs or assigns the

one half of the said estate, all the profit which shall or may arise from the said one half forever. In confirmation whereof I have hereunto set my hand and affixed my seal this 30th day of March 1773.
Signed sealed and delivered in presence of us William Dolman
Augustine Sanford
John Sanford
Richard Muse
At a court held for Westmoreland County the 30th day of March 1773 this deed of gift was acknowledged by William Dolman party thereto and ordered to be recorded. Test

Page 261.
William Carpenter's Nuncupative Will
Westmoreland to wit; Thomas Collinsworth and Sarah Williams of lawful age, being first sworn, deposeth and sayeth that they were at the house of William Carpenter on Tuesday the 23rd instant who lay ill but in sound and disposing sense and memory, and that he called on them to take notice that it was his will and desire that in case of his death, that his sister, Ann Carpenter should have his estate sold, and his just debts paid, and whatever might remain he gave to his said sister Ann Carpenter; and further that the said Carpenter did about 2 o'clock in the evening on the next day as near as they could guess, and further sayeth not. Thomas Collinsworth
The above sworn to 10 o'clock 24th March 1773 before Sarah Williams (her mark)
John Augustine Washington
At a court continued and held for Westmoreland County the 31st day of March 1773, this writing purporting the nuncupative will of William Carpenter, deceased, was proved according to law by the oaths of Thomas Collinsworth and Sarah Williams the witnesses thereto and ordered to be recorded; and on the motion of Thomas Blane who made oath thereto according to law, and together with Thomas Fisher his security entered into and acknowledged bond with condition as the law directs, certificate is granted him for obtaining letters of administration of the estate of the said decedent with the said will annexed in due form. Teste

Page 262.
McCarty to Sanford Indenture
This indenture made the 25th day of May 1773 between Daniel McCarty and Winifred McCarty his wife of the Parish of Washington and County of Westmoreland of the one part and Edward Sanford of the Parish of Cople and County of Westmoreland of the other part. Witnesseth that Daniel McCarty and Winifred McCarty his wife in consideration of 60 pounds current money has sold unto Edward Sanford all the tract of land lying in the Parish of Cople and County of Westmoreland upon the branches of Nominy River, bounded by the lands formerly known by the lands of William Sturman, and Thomas Stone, Thomas Sanford and Richard Sanford, Michael Robinson, William Sturman, Ashton & McCarty, containing by estimation 200 acres. In witness whereof the said Daniel McCarty and Winifred McCarty his wife have hereunto set their hands and seals the day and year above written.
Signed sealed and delivered in the presence of Daniel McCarty
Philip Smith Winifred McCarty
Benjamin Weeks
Benjamin Strother
To Benjamin Weeks and Philip Smith of the County of Westmoreland, Gent. Whereas Daniel McCarty of the Parish of Washington and County of Westmoreland, Gent., and Winifred McCarty his wife by their indenture of bargain and sale bearing date the 25th day of May 1773, have sold and conveyed unto Edward Sanford of the Parish of Cople and County aforesaid, the fee simple estate of a tract of land containing 200 acres lying in the said Parish of Cople and County aforesaid and whereas the said Winifred McCarty cannot

conveniently travel to our court to make acknowledgment. Therefore, we do give unto you or any two or more of you power to receive the acknowledgment which the said Winifred McCarty shall be willing to make for you of the conveyance. Witness James Davenport, clerk of our said court the 24th day of May 1773.
Westmoreland Sct. Pursuant to the above writ to us directed, we privy examined Mrs. Winifred McCarty spouse of Daniel McCarty apart from her husband and received her acknowledgement of the above-mentioned deed. Given under our hands this 25th day of May 1773.
At a court held for Westmoreland County the 25th day of May 1773, this indenture and receipt endorsed were proved by the oaths of Philip Smith, Benjamin Weeks, and Benjamin Strother the witnesses thereto and together with the commission annexed for taking the acknowledgment and privy examination of Winifred the wife of Daniel McCarty party thereto and a certificate of the execution thereof ordered to be recorded. Teste

Page 264.
Thomas Taylor's Will
In the name of God, Amen, I Thomas Taylor of the Parish of Washington and the County of Westmoreland being sick and weak in body but in perfect sense and memory do make and ordain this my last will and testament in the manner and form following;
Item I give unto Jeane Burne wife to Thomas Burne, one cow and calf.
Item I give unto Judith Stephens, one young heifer.
Item I give unto Lilly John Stephens, to him and his heirs, all my Negroes; Peter, Milly and Winny; and after my debts and funeral expenses are paid the said Lilly John Stephens shall have all the rest of my estate.
I constitute and appoint Lilly John Stephens executor to this my last will and testament. In witness whereof I have hereunto set my hand and seal this 25th day of September 1768.
Signed sealed and acknowledged in presence of. Thomas Taylor
Spence Monroe, Benjamin Stuart
John Atwood
At a court held for Westmoreland County the 25th day of May 1773 this will was proved according to law by the oaths of Benjamin Stuart and John Atwood witnesses thereto and ordered to be recorded; and on the motion of Lilly John Stephens the executor therein named who made oath thereto according to law and together with Benjamin Stuart and Woffendall Kendall his securities entered into and acknowledged bond with condition as the law directs, certificate is granted him for obtaining a probate thereof in due form. Teste

Page 265.
Gray to Gray Deed of Gift
This indenture made this [blank] day of April 1773 between Francis Gray of the Parish of Washington and County of Westmoreland of the one part and Nathaniel Gray, eldest son and heir at law of the said Francis Gray of the other part. Witnesseth that Francis Gray in consideration of the natural love and affection which he bears to Nathaniel Gray his son, hath given unto the said Nathaniel Gray all the tract of land with its appurtenances on which the said Francis Gray now resides lying in the parish and county aforesaid upon Rozier's Creek, containing 500 acres; and bounded southerly by Rozier's Creek, easterly by the lands of George Weedon and northerly and westerly by the lands of Capt. James Blair, deceased, together with the following slaves; Aron, Bob, Tom, Junior, Jessious, Sall, Milly, Cate, Winny, Surein? ; and all houses, outhouses, orchards and premises belonging. In witness whereof the said Francis Gray hath hereunto set his hand and seal the day and year first above written.
Signed sealed and delivered in presence of Francis Gray
William Strother, Thomas Canfield (his mark)
John Bryan, Sr.

At a court held for Westmoreland County the 25th day of May 1773 this indenture was proved by the oaths of William Strother, Thomas Canfield and John Bryan, Sr., the witnesses thereto and ordered to be recorded. Test James Davenport Cl Cl

Page 266.
Corbin to Corbin Deed of Gift
I Gawin Corbin of the Parish of St. Mary's and County of Caroline in consideration of the natural love and affection which I have and bear unto my dear sister, Miss Jane Corbin of Cople Parish and the County of Westmoreland, and also of for other good causes and considerations me thereunto moving have given by these presents mullato girl Lettice, about 18 years of age with her increase. But in case my sister should die without issue then the said Lettice and her increase to return to me. In witness whereof I have hereunto set my hand and seal this first day of January 1773.
Signed sealed in the presence of Gawin Corbin
John Turberville, Thomas Thompson
George Shoats, John Schon
At a court held for Westmoreland County the 25th day of May 1773 this deed of gift was proved by the oaths of John Turberville, Thomas Thompson and George Shoats witnesses thereto and ordered to be recorded. Teste

Page 267.
Turberville to Gill Lease
This indenture made the 15th day of April 1773 between John Turberville of the County of Westmoreland, Gent., of the one part and George Gill of the Parish of Cople in County of Westmoreland, planter of the other part. Witnessed that John Turberville in consideration of the rents and covenants herein after to be performed hath demised and to farm let unto George Gill one tenement of land containing by estimation 150 acres lying in the Parish of Cople and County of Westmoreland and bounded as follows; beginning at a marked red oak standing near the top of the Fulling Mill Hill and the line of Edward Gill's tenement, running a westerly course, a straight line to a mulberry and hickory tree growing from one stump and locked into each other, standing on a point between the first and second branches from the said Edward Gill's line, thence westerly from the said mulberry and hickory, down to the said second branch, thence southerly down the said second branch it several meanders down to the main branch being the head of Nominy mill pond, thence down the said pond as Sorrell's land runs as far as far as the corner, thence North along the said Sorrell's line to the edge of the swamp, between John Augustine Washington's mill pond, thence east along the said edge of the swamp and mill pond up to the corner between Edward Gill's land and Sorrell's, thence southerly along the said Edward Gill's line to the beginning marked red oak; it being part of the land the said John Turberville lately purchased of Thomas Sorrell. To have and to hold the said tenement with all appurtenances for and during the term of natural lives of George Gill and Ann Gill his wife and to the longest liver of them, yielding and paying unto John Turberville every year during the said term on the 25th day of December if demanded the need quantity of 1250 pounds of good crop tobacco (all leaf) and cask the said tobacco to be paid at such convenient warehouse in the said County of Westmoreland as the law from time to time shall appoint or direct for the payment of tobacco debts and the quit rents; and three fat geese or turkeys or 6 fat pullets or young cocks or six fat wild ducks every year during the said term. Lastly, the said George Gill and Ann Gill doth oblige themselves to build a good dwelling house, and plant an orchard of at least 500 peach trees on the said demised premises between the date of these presents and the end of December next and keep the orchard under a good and close fence. In witness whereof the parties within named to these presents have hereunto interchangeably set their hands and seals the day and year first within written.
Signed sealed and delivered in presence of John Turberville

Edward Gill George Gill
John Schon
At a court held for Westmoreland County the 25th day of May 1773 this indenture of lease was acknowledged by John Turberville and George Gill parties thereto and ordered to be recorded. Teste

Page 271.
Collingsworth to Crenshaw Indenture
This indenture made the 25th day of May 1773 between Thomas Collinsworth the County of Westmoreland of the one part and David Crenshaw of the Parish of Cople and County of Westmoreland, planter of the other part. Witnessed that Thomas Collinsworth in consideration of the rents and covenants to be performed hath demised and to farm let and to David Crenshaw one tenement of land containing by estimation 50 acres lying in the Parish of Cople and County of Westmoreland and bounded as follows; beginning at a marked white oak corner tree between Thomas Collinsworth and John Brinnon, standing in line of Jesse Collinsworth at the side of the swamp and running as the swamp runs a westerly course, to the head of the creek and thence as the creek runs the North course to a marked red oak corner tree at the line of John Collinsworth and thence an easterly straight line to a marked red oak stump at the road that leads to Nathaniel Butler's plantation, and thence a South East course as the road runs to a marked holly tree joining the line of John Brinnon and thence a South course a straight line to the first mentioned marked white oak; it being part of the land the said Thomas Collinsworth now holds in possession. To have and to hold the said tenement and premises unto the said David Crenshaw during the term of 10 years yielding and paying 100 pounds Virginia currency as follows; 10 pounds at the acknowledgment of this indenture, 10 pounds the first day of January 1774; at which time the said David Crenshaw is to take the land in possession and then to be clear of paying any rent till the first day of January 1777 at which time the next rent of 10 pounds shall become due, only half the expense of breaking the entail of the said land to be deducted from it, and the other half to be deducted from the next years rent of 10 pounds which expenses the said David Crenshaw is to be at when required which rent last mentioned will become due the first day of January 1778, and the said David Crenshaw doth oblige themselves to pay 10 pounds a year till the date of 1784 is expired. In witness whereof the parties within named to these presents have hereunto interchangeably set their hands and seals the day and year first above written.
Signed and sealed in the presence of Thomas Collinsworth
George Curtis, George Gill David Crenshaw
John Brinnon, Jr.
At a court held for Westmoreland County the 25th day of May 1773 this indenture of lease was acknowledged by Thomas Collinsworth and David Crenshaw parties thereto and ordered to be recorded. Teste

Page 273.
Brown & Hutt Articles of Agreement
Articles of agreement indented made concluded and agreed upon this third day of April 1773 between William Brown of the Parish of Cople in County of Westmoreland of the one part and Gerard Hutt of the same Parish and County aforesaid of the other part. Witnessed that whereas William Brown and Gerard Hutt have mutually agreed to build a water grist mill at joint expense and in the place where George Brown, deceased, formerly had a mill and bequeathed the same to Priscilla Fryer and her heirs forever as will appear by his last will bearing date the 18th day of May 1724.
Now the true interpretation and meaning of these presents are that the proposed mill should be erected at the place aforesaid to which are to be added 1 acre of land at each end of the dam, to the mill aforesaid and all the land that is laid underwater by the erecting of this mill is

to be valued by Mr. Solomon Redman and Mr. Thomas Edwards, Gent., One half of which valuation is to be paid by the said Gerard Hutt, to the said William Brown as the land that will be covered with water belongs to the said William Brown. It is also agreed upon the parties that every expense attending the building and erecting the said mill and keeping her in good repair shall be at their joint expense and all the profit that arises by the building the said mill is to be equally divided between them as long as the mill continues and that the said Gerard Hutt is to have a fee simple estate in the mill but the aforesaid Gerard Hutt obliges themselves not to sell his right of the said mill without the consent of the said William Brown; and the said William Brown shall at all times if they choose, the liberty of furnishing the mill with a miller; one of his or their own servants or slaves as they shall think proper, shall find the said miller proper clothing such as our usual for servants or Negroes to wear, and pay his life and find him sufficient diet, and the said Gerard Hutt shall pay to the said William Brown in current money of Virginia on the first day of January annually from the date above mentioned as long as they shall continue in partnership in the said mill, one half of the value of the miller's clothing, live and diet and also ½ hire of the said miller; according to the custom of hiring Negroes annually, and the said Gerard Hutt shall not at any time be allowed to keep any sows, pigs, shoats, or hogs at the aforesaid mill or on any part of the land thereto belonging. To the true performance of the above articles each party binds himself each to the other in the full and just sum of 500 pounds current money of Virginia. In witness whereof the parties aforesaid have to this indenture set their hands and seals the day and year first above written.
Signed sealed and delivered in presence of us William Brown
John Smith Gerard Hutt
Vincent Redman
George McKenney
At a court held for Westmoreland County the 25th day of May 1773 these articles of agreement were acknowledged by William Brown and Gerard Hutt parties thereto and ordered to be recorded. Test

Page 275.
Sanford & Wife to Davenport Indenture
This indenture made the 25th day of May 1773 between Joel Sanford of the Parish of Cople and County of Westmoreland, planter and Jemima Sanford his wife of the one part and James Davenport of the same parish and county, Gent., of the other part. Witnesseth that Joel Sanford and Jemima Sanford his wife in consideration of 110 pounds current money have sold to James Davenport all that tract of land containing about 109 acres whereon the said Joel Sanford now liveth lying in the parish and county aforesaid, adjoining to and binding on the lands of Edward Ransdell, Alexander Spark, Solomon Redman and Edward Sanford. In witness whereof the said Joel Sanford and Jemima Sanford have hereunto set their hands and affixed their seals the day and year above written.
Sealed and delivered in presence of Joel Sanford
David Boyd, James Sorrell Jemima Sanford (her mark)
Peter Rust
At a court held for Westmoreland County the 25th day of May 1773 this indenture was acknowledged by Joel Sanford and Jemima his wife parties thereto (she being first privy examinded as the law directs) and ordered to be recorded. Teste

Page 277.
Graham & Wife to Jordan Indenture
this indenture made the 10th day of May 1773 between John Augustine Washington, Esq. of Cople Parish in the County of Westmoreland and in the colony of Virginia, attorney for and duly authorized by William Campbell and Betty Campbell his wife of Fairfield, of the County of Ayr in North Britain and John Graham and Elizabeth Graham his wife of Northumberland

County in the colony of Virginia the one part and Reuben Jordan of Cople Parish in County of Westmoreland and colony of Virginia aforesaid of the other part. Witnessed that John Augustine Washington, Esq. Attorney for the said William Campbell and Betty Campbell his wife in the said John Graham and Elizabeth Graham his wife in consideration of 50 pounds current money of Virginia have sold to Reuben Jordan all that tract of land lying in the Parish of Cople and County of Westmoreland in the forest of Nominy, on or near one of the head branches of Nominy River, containing by estimation 150 acres, and is part of a patent for 1000 acres of land granted to William Basely and Edward Hawley bearing date the 22nd day of March 1665, one half of which said patent was by the said Edward Hawley sold and assigned to Martin Cole, and was by the said Martin Cole sold and assigned to Richard Tidwell and Robert Jeffries, and the said Richard Tidwell and Robert Jeffries sold and disposed of all the above moiety being 500 acres of land, except the above mentioned 150 acres, which became the property of the said Richard Tidwell, son of Richard Tidwell who sold and conveyed the same to William Metcalfe as by deeds of lease and release bearing date the 26th and 27th days of September 1721; and the said William Metcalfe dying intestate, the same descended to and became the fee simple estate of his two daughters, Ann Metcalfe and Betty Metcalfe as coheirs who intermarried, the first with Mr. John Graham, deceased and the other with the said William Campbell, and the said John Graham and Ann Graham his wife dying intestate and without disposing of their part of the said 150 acres of land, then the same became the fee simple estate of the said John Graham party to these presents and the said William Campbell and Betty Campbell his wife by their certain power of attorney bearing date the 10th day of April 1771 authorizing the said John Augustine Washington, Esq. full power to dispose of their part of the said 150 acres of land. In witness whereof the first parties to these presents have interchangeably set their hands and seals the day and year first above written.

Signed sealed and delivered in presence of
Joseph Lane
John Sinclair
George Steptoe
Hugh Hamilton
Richard Lee

John Augustine Washington
attorney for William Campbell and
Betty Campbell his wife

To Lindsay Opie, William Eskridge and Kenner Cralle of the County of Northumberland, Gent. Whereas Rev John Augustine Washington, Esq., attorney for and duly authorized by William Campbell and Betty Campbell his wife of Ayr in Great Britain and John Graham and Elizabeth his wife of Northumberland County, by their indenture of bargain and sale. Dated the 10th day of May 1773 have sold and County and to Reuben Jordan the fee simple estate of 150 acres of land lying in the Parish of Cople and County of Westmoreland, and whereas the said Elizabeth Graham cannot conveniently travel to our court to make acknowledgment. Therefore, we do give unto you or any two or more of you power to receive the acknowledgement which the said Elizabeth Graham shall be willing to make. Witness James Davenport, clerk of our court the 10th day of 1773.

Northumberland County Sct. By virtue of the above writ to us directed we did personally go to Elizabeth Graham wife of John Graham and did examine her apart of her husband and she acknowledged the indenture hereunto annexed to be her act and deed and that she did the same freely and voluntarily without persuasions or threats of her husband and was willing that the same should be recorded in the County Court of Westmoreland. All of which we do hereby certify under our hands and seals this 11th day of May 1773.

Lindsay Opie
William Eskridge

At a court held for Westmoreland County the 29th day of June 1773 this indenture and the receipt endorsed proved as to John Graham and Elizabeth Graham his wife by the oath of Richard Lee, Esq. a witness thereto and having been proved by the oaths of Joseph Lane and John Sinclair two other of the witnesses thereto and the same were acknowledged by

John Augustine Washington, Esq., attorney for William Campbell and Betty Campbell his wife and together with the commission annexed for taking the acknowledgment and privy examination the said Elizabeth Graham and a certificate of the execution thereof ordered to be recorded. Teste

Page 281.
Turberville to Taylor Lease
This indenture made the 31st day of October 1771 between John Turberville of the County of Westmoreland, Gent., of the one part and Thomas Taylor of the Parish of Cople and County of Westmoreland, planter of the other part. Witnesseth that John Turberville in consideration of the rents and covenants has demised and to farm let unto Thomas Taylor a tenement of land containing 100 acres lying in the Parish of Cople and County of Westmoreland and bounded as followeth; beginning at the corner line between the land of the Hon. Robert Carter and Robert Middleton, deceased, from thence a straight line to the mouth of Crabbs Road?, thence a straight line along the Narrows Road to the upper part of the said Taylor's cleared ground, thence along the said cleared ground to Yeocomico Creek, thence along the said creek to Middleton's line, thence along the said Middleton's line, to the beginning. To have and to hold the said tenement with all appurtenances unto the said Thomas Taylor for and during the natural lives of him the said Thomas Taylor and Mary Taylor his now wife to the survivor and the longest liver of them, yielding and paying yearly and every year during the term on the 25th day of December, if demanded, the net quantity of 1250 pounds of good tobacco and cask the said tobacco to be paid at such convenient warehouse in the said County of Westmoreland as the law from time to time shall appoint for the payment of tobacco debts and the quit rents, and two fat geese; and they will build a tobacco house 32' x 20' and will keep an orchard of 500 good peach trees and 100 good apple trees under a good close fence. In witness whereof the parties within named to these presents have hereunto interchangeably set their hands and seals the day and year first written.
Signed sealed and delivered in presence of John Turberville
William Omohundro Thomas Taylor (his mark)
Byron Stonum
At a court held for Westmoreland County the 29th day of June 1773 this indenture of lease was acknowledged by John Turberville and Thomas Taylor parties thereto and ordered to be recorded. Teste

Page 284.
Lee to Self Indenture
This indenture made the 23rd day of November 1771 between Richard Lee, Esq. the one part and Stephen Self, Jr., of the other part. Witnesseth that Richard Lee in consideration of the rents and covenants has demised and to farm let one tenement of land now in the tenure in occupation of the said Stephen Self containing 100 acres, adjoining the lands of Philip Smith, Fleet Cox, George Fairfax Lee, and on the upper side of the branch above Hollidays lease. To have and to hold the said tenement of land with appurtenances from the day of the date hereof in during the natural life of the said Stephen Self, yielding and paying yearly in every year during the said term, the rent of one thousand pounds of crop tobacco and cask and the quit rents on the 25th day of December yearly; and to leave standing in some convenient part of the above granted premises in one body at least 30 acres of woods untouched which woods shall remain in be held as a further support of the plantation and form; and further within the space of two years build or cause to build on the demised lands a good dwelling house 20' x 16', a 30 foot tobacco house, and a corner house or other houses and buildings equal thereto; and plant an orchard of 100 winter apple trees at 30 foot distance away from each other and 100 peach trees at 15 feet distance from each other. In witness whereof the said parties have hereunto interchangeably set their hands and affixed their seals the day month and year first above written.

Signed sealed and delivered in the presence of Richard Lee
Reuben Jordan Stephen Self, Jr.
At a court held for Westmoreland County the 29th day of June 1773 this indenture of lease was acknowledged by Richard Lee and Stephen Self, Jr., parties thereto and ordered to be recorded. Teste

Page 289.
Steptoe to Lowe Indenture
This indenture made this 30th day of May 1773 between Dr. George Steptoe of the County of Westmoreland, Gent., of the one part and Richard Lowe of the county aforesaid, planter of the other part. Witnesseth that George Steptoe in consideration of 183 pounds, 6 shillings, and 8 pence has sold to Richard Lowe all that part of land where the said Richard Lowe now lives being the land laid off by Samuel Rust, Jeremiah Rust and Fleet Cox by order of Westmoreland County for Mrs. Griffin's dower. Beginning at a red oak a corner tree in William Jeffries line, thence South 44 poles to a gum, a corner to Richard Lowe's land, thence South 65° West 32 poles, to a small white oak, thence South 74° West 70 poles to a large beech on the Spring Branch, then down the Spring Branch to the creek, then up the meanders of the creek to a small pine at the creek side, and from thence to the beginning, supposed to contain 100 acres. In witness whereof the said parties to these presents have interchangeably set their hands and seals the day and year first above written.
Sealed and delivered in presence of George Steptoe
James Walker, Alexander Cunningham
Thomas Fisher, Hugh Hamilton
At a court held for Westmoreland County the 27th day of July 1773 this indenture of feoffment together with the memorandum of livery of seizen thereon endorsed proved by the oaths of Alexander Cunningham, Thomas Fisher and Hugh Hamilton witnesses thereto and ordered to be recorded. Teste

Page 291.
James Berryman's Will
In the name of God, Amen, I James Berryman of the County of Westmoreland and Parish of Washington do make and ordain this my last will and testament in manner and form following.
First, I give to my son James Berryman all the land I bought of William Neale in the province of Maryland, but in case he should die before he arrives of age or marries then to my son Samuel Berryman and his heirs, and in failure of such heirs then to be sold and divided between my three daughters Caty Berryman, Frances Berryman and Sarah Berryman.
Secondly, the land I bought of John Welch, I leave to be sold in order to pay off my debts.
Thirdly, all the rest of my estate of Negroes, stocks, household goods &c., I leave to be equally divided between my four sons and three daughters; John Berryman, James Berryman, Samuel Berryman, Newton Berryman, Caty Berryman, Frances Berryman and Sarah Berryman or their survivors.
Fourthly, in case all my children should die without heirs I give my whole estate, lands, Negroes &c., to my loving wife Sarah Berryman, she not been debarred of her thirds as the law directs.
Fifthly, my will is that my estate may not be appraised.
Sixthly, I constitute and appoint my loving wife Sarah Berryman, my whole sole executrix this my last will and testament. In witness whereof I have hereunto set my hand and seal this 25th day of January 1772.
Signed sealed and acknowledged in the presence of James Berryman
James Newman
George Kitchen
Joseph Lane

At a court held for Westmoreland County the 27th day of July 1773 this will was proved according to law by the oaths of James Newman, George Kitchen and Joseph Lane the witnesses thereto and ordered to be recorded and on the motion of Sarah Berryman the executrix therein named who made oath thereto according to law and together with Samuel Dishman her security entered into and acknowledged bond with condition as the law directs, certificate is granted her for obtaining a probate thereof in due form. Teste

Page 292.
Moxley to Dolman Indenture & Performance Bond
This indenture made the 27th day July 1773 between Augustine Moxley of the Parish of Cople and County of Westmoreland of the one part and Sarah Dolman of the aforesaid Parish and County of the other part. Witnesseth that Augustine Moxley in consideration of 265 pounds, one shilling current money of Virginia has sold to Sarah Dolman all his right title and interest into a certain piece or dividend of land (1/2 acre where the graveyard is only excepted) containing by estimation 171 acres, situate in the said Parish of Cople and County of Westmoreland, and bounded as followeth; beginning at a marked white oak near the swamp and running a line by the said white oak dividing this land from that of John Washington to a marked walnut, from thence to a white oak corner to the said Washington's and Joseph Moxley, thence along the said Moxley's line to a small marked poplar standing in the head of a branch, thence down the said branch to another [branch] falling into this, thence to a small hickory standing on a point, thence to a white oak on the ridge path, being a corner tree to Augustine Sanford and Joseph Moxley, and from that to the beginning as the plot a appears.
In witness whereof the said parties to these presents have interchangeably set their hands and seals the day month and year first above written.
Signed sealed and delivered in the presence of us Augustine Moxley
Augustine Sanford
William Omohundro
Youell Sanford
At a court held for Westmoreland County the 27th day of July 1773 this indenture of feoffment together with the memorandum of livery of seizen and receipt endorsed were acknowledge five Augustine Moxley party thereto and ordered to be recorded. Teste
Performance bond executed same day by Augustine Moxley and Elizabeth Moxley his wife.

Page 296.
Critcher & Wife to Rochester Indenture
This indenture made the 28th day of September 1773 between Thomas Critcher and Easter Critcher his wife of the County of Granville and province of North Carolina of the one part and John Rochester of the County of Westmoreland and colony of Virginia of the other part. Witnesseth that Thomas Critcher and Easter [Hester] Critcher in consideration of 80 pounds current money of Virginia has sold to John Rochester a tract of land lying in the Parish of Cople in County of Westmoreland containing by estimation 100 acres and bounded as followeth; on the lands of the Hon. Robert Carter, Esq., on the lands of John Simpson, and on the lands of the said John Rochester, which he purchased of Gerald Hutt, it being the land whereof the said Thomas Critcher formerly lived and his wife's dower from her late husband John Rochester, deceased and the land whereupon the said John Rochester now lives.
In witness whereof the first parties to these presents have interchangeably set their hands and seals the day and year first above written.
Signed sealed and delivered in presence of Easter Critcher
Peter Brickey
Hugh Thomas
At a court held for Westmoreland County the 28th day of September 1773 this indenture was acknowledged by Easter Critcher the wife of Thomas Critcher (she being first privy examined as the law directs) and ordered to be recorded. Test

www.ingramcontent.com/pod-product-compliance
Lightning Source LLC
LaVergne TN
LVHW061250100826
845148LV00008B/1086